HEAD OVER HEELS

HEAD OVER HEELS

A CELEBRATION of BRITISH FOOTBALL

AUTHOR
JIM HOSSACK

———•———

INTRODUCTION
DON REVIE

MAINSTREAM
PUBLISHING

This book is dedicated to everyone who has the welfare of football in their heart. To those great players of yesteryear who made the game and to the memory of the Rev. Arthur Gray . . . football fan and humanitarian.

Copyright © Jim Hossack, 1989

First published in Great Britain 1989 by
MAINSTREAM PUBLISHING COMPANY (EDINBURGH) LTD
7 Albany Street
Edinburgh EH1 3UG

ISBN 1 85158 209 6 (cloth)
ISBN 1 85158 210 X (paper)

British Library Cataloguing in Publication Data

Hossack, Jim
  Head over heels . . .: a celebration of British
  football.
  1. Great Britain. Association football, to 1983
  I. Title
  796.334′0941

  ISBN 1-85158-209-6
  ISBN 1-85158-210-X pbk

Typeset in 11 on 13pt Times by Blackpool Typesetting Services Ltd, Blackpool.
Printed in Great Britain by Richard Clay Ltd, Bungay, Suffolk.

CONTENTS

ACKNOWLEDGEMENTS

The author wishes to thank the following for their assistance and encouragement.

Ian Armour, Agnes Arnott, Larry Canning, Beth Cummings, Paul Daniels, Ken Dodds, Ricky Fearon, Fred Fullagar, Michael Gray, Lord Hailsham of St. Marylebone, John Hamilton, Tony Higgins, Pat Higney, Ian Lamont, Pat Lamont, John Melrose, Joe Mercer, Charlie Mullen, George McGhee, Bob Patience, Ronnie Paterson, Allan Pender, The Scottish Tourist Board, The *Sunday Mail*, Jason Tomas and Robert Wallace.

A very special thankyou to the *Glasgow Herald*, in particular Harry Reid and Jim McNeish, for permission to use many of the *Herald's* marvellous photographs within the pages of this book.

AUTHOR'S NOTE

Over the years football has meant a tremendous amount to me. I owe a huge debt of personal gratitude to those marvellous players whose skills have greatly enriched my life.

It, therefore, gives me immense pleasure to donate my ENTIRE share of the profits from this 'labour of love' to The Scottish Professional Footballer's Association.

S.P.F.A. Secretary, Tony Higgins, a great pal whom I hold in the highest possible esteem, will, I know, use the money wisely . . . and, in doing so, be ever mindful of the enormous and priceless contribution which those wonderful footballing 'giants' of yesteryear made to our glorious game!

Jim Hossack
July 1989

INTRODUCTION
by Don Revie

I regard it as an honour to have been given the opportunity to write the introduction to this book, partly because Jim Hossack is one of the most remarkable football followers I have ever come across.

I first met him before a Scotland-England match at Hampden five or six years ago, and was immediately struck by his enthusiasm for the game and, more specifically, his affection for the stars who graced it during the glorious, halcyon days of the past. In the 1940s and 1950s, stars like Wilf Mannion and

George Young did much to attract and enthral capacity crowds wherever they played. But, under the restriction of the maximum wage, their financial rewards were pitiful in comparison with those of their counterparts today. Indeed, many have fallen on hard times. It's a situation which has long rankled with me, as it has with Jim Hossack. He has devoted an enormous amount of time in striving to help the golden names of yesteryear.

It has become an obsession.

It is not difficult to appreciate why.

Most people who watched matches in the immediate post-war eras will agree that the game in Britain, while having become more professional, is nowhere near as entertaining. Players have become stronger physically, and quicker. The game is now played at break-neck speed, and the precious few players who can be termed the modern equivalents of the Mannions don't get the same scope to express their talents.

I am often asked how the great players of the 1940s and 1950s would fare in today's game. I am convinced that they would adjust to it . . . but they wouldn't stand out as much. That's sad. There have been enormous social and economic changes in Britain over the last forty to fifty years. But one aspect of football which remains the same is the desire of spectators to see players producing exciting, creative skills. There are no longer enough genuine stars, and that goes some way towards explaining why the game has lost so much of its appeal. It also explains why, like Jim Hossack, I still cherish the memories that the great footballers of the past gave me.

Take Mannion, my boyhood idol. I lived close to the Middlesbrough ground and, most weekday mornings, Mannion and the other Middlesbrough players would pass by my street on their way to Ayresome Park for training. I'd make a point of being there to watch him go by, and I lost count the number of times I got his autograph. I still vividly recall the effect he had on the Middlesbrough crowd when he got his first touch of the ball. The whole place erupted. He had a wide repertoire of ball-playing skills, the most notable of which was his tendency to throw opponents off balance by passing his foot over the ball.

Another player who created millions of boyhood fantasies was Stan Matthews. Even when I played with him in the England team, he did things which made the hair at the back of my neck stand up. Remember England's 7-2 win over Scotland at Wembley in 1955? He beat Scotland virtually on his own that day. I was his inside-forward partner, and early in the game hit a pass to him that was both too hard and too high. Matthews just lifted a foot and caressed the ball out of the air as if controlling it with a magnet. I just shook my head and thought: "Bloody Hell, *what* skill!"

Jim Hossack was presented with a prestigious merit award at the Scottish Professional Footballers' Association dinner in 1987. His concern for the welfare of the stars of the past and his personal love of the game was duly recognised, and is emphasised in this intriguing book.

Jim's words come from the heart and reach out to the very soul of the game.

AUTHOR'S NOTE

Sadly, having written the introduction to this publication, Don Revie passed away in May 1989, after a courageous two-year battle against the cruel and, as yet, incurable Motor Neurone disease.

Don was a big man in every sense. Brave, warm-hearted and caring, he was a first-class footballer and one of the finest managers in the history of the sport. To know him was a great privilege, not because a catalogue of remarkable achievements transformed the man into a football legend but, much more importantly, because big Don was one of the nicest and kindest human beings that it has been my good fortune to encounter. Immensely thankful that our paths crossed, I shall forever cherish memories of a genius, a man whom his "family" of internationally famous Leeds United players, such as Jack Charlton, Billy Bremner, Eddie Gray, Johnny Giles and Peter Lorimer, simply idolised and affectionately called "Boss" to the very end.

Typically, despite his terrible illness, Don Revie found the time and energy to write the introduction to this book. Though I am greatly honoured, it is the source of immense personal sadness that Don is not here to see his words in print.

Kevin Keegan, that wonderful player and former England captain, summed up the feelings of many when, at Don Revie's funeral, he said: "Mr Revie was like a father to me, a very special man whom it was a privilege to know. He saved my England career, and I have tremendous memories of him. He was a great manager."

1

THE GAMES WE PLAYED AS LADDIES

When I was a lad and huge crowds packed the terracings!

When I was a lad and magical players, not coaches in dug-outs or legislators in ivory towers, were the life-blood of the game!

When I was a lad and every team in the land boasted five attack-minded forwards!

When I was a little lad, life was an indescribable dream, neatly wrapped in an all-embracing love affair with football!

''That boy is far from stupid. If he really puts his mind to it he could become a doctor, a lawyer, or even a brain surgeon . . . but he's allowing an idiotic obsession with football to threaten his future prospects.'' Many years later my father's despairing words to my late, dear mother still echo in my ears. My parents' early anxiety was wholly understandable, because the game was all that really mattered to me. But they needn't have worried and, if truth be known, they fully understood where the root cause of that obsession lay.

In 1949, at the age of three and a half, I contracted polio which, thankfully, left me paralysed down the left side of my face. I say ''thankfully'' because my limbs were unaffected and I am indebted to my lucky stars for that. Since then I have undergone many plastic surgery operations but, in the long-gone days of the 1950s, I must have looked a bit like a stunted version of an extra from a Hammer horror film.

However, as they say, beauty is really only skin deep, isn't it? Nevertheless a rhino-like hide was required to cope with the constant mocking of some of my school-mates. The playground can be an extremely cruel and hostile environment if you happen, through no fault of your own, to be that little bit different. Perhaps that explains why I enjoyed Charles Laughton's (not Tommy Lawton's) portrayal of Quasimodo, the crippled bellringer, in the classic film *The Hunchback of Notre Dame*. Maybe I was able to identify with his plight a little more closely than most and to fully appreciate why the poor soul sought sanctuary and hid himself away within the dark cloisters of that great cathedral. My sanctuary was sought in the wonderful world of football. A fantasy world full of cascading dreams and aspirations. A colourful mental kaleidoscope with ever-changing images which provided a much needed protective cushion from the stinging jibes and thoughtless taunts of the mob.

But I had some friends . . . kindred spirits who shared a tremendous passion for this greatest of games. We were a mischievous little band which, regularly and stealthily, crawled under the turnstiles at Love Street in Paisley, minds boggling in anticipation at the thought of the money to be earned from empty beer bottles collected on the terracing, eyes agog, while gazing up in wonder and total adoration at the galaxy of star players who came and went every other Saturday at St Mirren's famous ground.

Like the majority of kids our heads were full of devilment. My mates and I rang more doorbells than most, supremely confident in our ability to run like the very wind when hotly pursued by some demented and long-suffering inhabitant. We were very much to the fore when the bools and conkers titles were being dished out and great pleasure was derived from pinching the girls' peevers and in doing everything possible to disrupt their futile attempts at skipping. Nobody scanned the personal ads in the local paper but, somehow, each of us knew instinctively just where and when every wedding was scheduled to take place in that home town of Renfrew. Howls of pain and the sound of crunching fingers could be heard as a best mate's hand was trampled underfoot in a selfish effort to gain possession of a highly prized threepenny bit lying invitingly among the pile of coppers scattered by the bride or groom. In Spring there was hardly a tadpole left swimming in the local pond and life was a joyous concoction of lucky bags, home-made bows and arrows, broken biscuits, cowboys and Indians, apple-stealing missions and endless happy hours spent in the "Bug Hut", which was the finest cinema to be found this side of Hollywood. It may not have been "amang the heather", but, as Sir Harry Lauder so poignantly sang: "The games we played as laddies, they will never be forgot."

All of these were marvellous pastimes, but the "be all and end all" of our young lives was football. What fun was had exchanging bubblegum and sweetie cigarette cards: "I'll gie you Roy Bentley for Trevor Ford . . . then I only need big Geordie Young and I've got the whole set." Shoes were scuffed out of recognition and beyond repair as we noisily pursued a tennis ball around the playground like a pack of half-starved mongrels scrapping over a bone, until the school bell compelled our sweaty band of heroes to return to the awful and unbelievable boredom that was school-work.

I never fully understood why so much priceless time had to be spent in that dingy Victorian classroom, in which generations of unfortunate children had suffered, while that dreary old crone of a teacher attempted to allocate a tiny corner of my mind to the meaningless things in life. Stupid, mundane things like arithmetic and English . . . subjects which were never going to be of the slightest benefit to me anyway. Surely it was a cruel and, indeed, criminal act to keep a soccer talent such as mine caged within the grey and forbidding walls of a school? After all, wasn't I going to become a professional footballer? Pen-pushing in some dreadful office just didn't figure in any long-term plans, because I was going to score more goals than Lawrie Reilly or Nat Lofthouse and would be idolised by millions. Every kid from John o' Groats to Land's End would be clamouring for an autograph and there was no disputing the fact that I was destined to become "King" of the sports pages, a hero who would hit both the net and the headlines with devastating, yet predictable, regularity. But all of that was in the future and in the meantime, though totally innocent of any crime against society, I just had to serve my sentence and come to terms with the fact that during most weekdays there were lengthy spells when imprisonment with torture simply had to be endured with little or no chance of premature escape.

But, come four o'clock, that same old school bell suddenly became sweet music to the ears because then, when temporarily liberated from the dreadful drudgery of that classroom dungeon, my jacket and others could form piles of makeshift goalposts, while our pint-sized gang of soccer stars played fitba' until pangs of hunger and a cloak of darkness sent us scurrying home to those anxious and long-suffering mums. There were no washing machines or spin driers in those days and not a passing thought was given to the heap of mud-spattered clothes which had to be washed by hand and fed through that old-fashioned wringer.

A *Roy of the Rovers* fan and a somewhat comical character in my own right, I had way-out dreams of waltzing through the entire England defence, rounding the goalie and scoring yet another glorious winning goal at Wembley. Yes . . . that highly fashionable English rear-guard were sold more dummies than could be found in the length and breadth of Carnaby Street as I teased, tricked and tormented Billy Wright's boys nightly in a stylish and tailor-made soccer career which stretched from bedtime to breakfast.

Coronations, ascents of Everest and the state of the nation never came to mind, as wee Jim speculated on the forthcoming Saturday's results or the prospects for the new season. I had simply no idea who the Secretary of State for Scotland was . . . who cared anyway? It could have been Humphrey Bogart. Maybe Sir Anthony Eden was the star of *Jack and the Beanstalk* at Glasgow's Alhambra Theatre. But I did know that Willie Waddell was Rangers' famous right-winger, that Stenhousemuir played at Ochilview and that a will-o'-the-wisp called Stanley Matthews had, almost single-handedly, won the English Cup for Blackpool. School-work may have been my weakest subject but, when it came to remembering football results, that little brain of mine was as sharp and incisive as any modern computer.

How can I ever forget those early matches at dear old Love Street, where the seeds of an incurable football malady were first sown? Echoing across the years comes the sound of thousands of pairs of frozen feet stamping in unison on an icy, winter terracing. The distinctive and pungent smell of countless sodden raincoats, mingling with the sweet and welcoming aroma of bubbling Bovril and hot pies wafting out from a refreshment hut suffocating in a cloud of steam. Many an autograph was collected on a discarded fag packet with a sticky, well-chewed pencil being eagerly and expectantly thrust into the hands of football's greatest names. Barrow-loads of fabulous goals were witnessed and a host of colourful and larger-than-life characters encountered at each and every match. Those crowds were liberally littered with Billy Connolly-style comedians and prolific patter merchants. How my pals and I giggled and chuckled with delight at the procession of humorous dialogue directed towards the players and the referee. Mind you, those amiable jokers could, within the space of a split second, erupt into passionate fury and turn into uninhibited, foul-mouthed madmen as an opposition defender sent one of their "fine lads" sprawling in the penalty box and that "f****** bampot" of a referee inexplicably waved . . . play on!

On leaving the ground, drowned in a sea of adult legs, we gradually channelled a furrow to the Renfrew-bound tram, clutching old coal sacks full of jingling bottles . . . rich pickings which, when exchanged for hard currency at the local pub, would ensure that each and every one of us could enjoy a jumbo-sized poke of the finest chips that money could buy when we got home . . . All in all an endless maze of wonder to an impressionable child!

Needless to say those dreams of personal glory on the football field, which had deftly danced across my imagination in such a confident and carefree fashion, didn't come to fruition and this lad never scored a goal at Wembley, or anywhere else of note for that matter. But I console myself in the sure and certain knowledge that "Jimmy boy" crashed many an unstoppable and dramatic "clincher" between those makeshift goalposts. Oh yes, football was, and indeed still is, a lovely, lovely game. It conjures up so many magical and vivid images of childhood. If only I had kept those marvellous autographs and sweetie cigarette cards. Why, oh why, was I daft enough to swap them for that long-broken catapult?

When the great day dawned and schooldays finally became a closed book, I embarked on a career in the television industry. My first job as a

Football . . . a world of wonder through the eyes of a child!

sixteen-year-old was that of an office boy on Scottish Television's nightly news-magazine programme, *Here And Now*. What an invigorating and memorable time that was. Commercial television was in its infancy and each day was filled with the expectation of meeting new and famous faces within the confines of a vibrant and exhilarating environment. Bing Crosby, The Beatles, Ella Fitzgerald, Frankie Vaughan, Sonny Liston . . . an endless list of star names rolled along to STV's studios in Glasgow's Theatre Royal to be greeted by the fresh-faced and starry-eyed lad which I was then. Jinking among the studio cameras when the "live" programme was "on air", dashing to and fro between the battery of offices and along the labyrinth of endless corridors that was the colourful Theatre Royal interior, mine was an exceedingly busy and happy existence. However, despite experiencing the ultimate in job satisfaction, Saturday, even in the depths of winter, was the day on which the sun forever shone. Let's face it! Who really wanted to converse with the likes of Crosby and Sean Connery, or even ogle at Sophia Loren, when the lure of the terracing tugged relentlessly at the heart-strings and the opportunity arose to "rub shoulders" with the greats of football, to share their disappointments and to bask contentedly in reflected glory when the results were to my liking? Those heroes of the soccer field were the true giants of showbusiness, because they portrayed a wide-ranging repertoire of talents on the greatest stages of all. When you really come to think about it, almost anybody could croon like Bing, tickle those piano keys as delicately as Russ Conway, or play Hamlet like Richard Burton. But it was only at football stadiums that the opportunity presented itself to witness the breath-taking skills of megastars such as Jim Baxter, Johnny Haynes and George Best.

But then, as now, for several weeks every year the curtain always came down on this glittering sporting extravaganza. Yes, horror of horrors . . . the close season!

The rarefied, strawberries-and-cream atmosphere of Wimbledon is simply no substitute for the bright lights of the annual football circus. During those lazy, hazy, crazy days of summer, when hibernation would surely present a realistic alternative, we've just got to make do with lesser sports like tennis and golf, to content ourselves with watching stars of the running track like Steve Cram and Seb Coe or the languid and boring antics of those podgy, so-called "heroes" of the cricket field. What a welcome the glorious month of August receives from fans starved of soccer for far too long. Team colours are taken out of mothballs yet again and we fitba' lads are in carnival mood, delighted to jump on to football's merry-go-round once more and to hurl ourselves on to the emotional helter-skelter of another hectic season.

Over the years my love affair with football, like Topsy, simply grew and grew. Hand in hand and seldom parted, the romance blossomed as the game steered me through many a personal crisis. Now in my forties and very happily married with three little sons (a half-back line), it's my wife, Margaret, who's convinced that I'm "a suitable case for treatment". She's "fed up" answering endless telephone calls . . . "Jim's away at Hampden, but I'll remind him to meet you at Dundee's ground tomorrow and make sure he brings a photograph of Bobby Moore." She's "tired" of opening the door to the postman who has called to deliver a bundle of the new season's Mansfield Town or Crewe Alexandra programmes and the dear lady "couldn't care less" about the fact that, in 1967, Celtic became the first British side to win the European Cup when they defeated Inter Milan 2-1 . . . and the legend of those "Lisbon Lions" was born!

For as long as I care to remember I have collected football memorabilia. Programmes, books, photographs, badges, anything remotely connected with the game. Our loft resembles a museum, an Aladdin's cave of personal treasures and mementos. What a haven that attic of mine provides. The cares of the outside world are forgotten in an environment which has provided a welcome refuge from the bullying boss as well as the beastly bank manager and a temporary hiding-place from the eternal din and hubbub of family life. An island of tranquillity in a sometimes choppy sea, it's a safe harbour from which I can slip anchor and sail away into the fascinating world of football.

What great pleasure I derive from those old programmes and souvenirs. They jog the memory and transport the mind back to happy days and to sad ones; to the 2,000-odd matches I have attended at ports of call from sunny Lisbon to a snow-swept Glebe Park in Brechin; but, most importantly of all, to those fabulous players who made the game and to their devoted fans. My long-suffering wife was horrified when the Glasgow *Evening Times* took an interest in my collection and published a feature in which they described me as "The Loony of the Loft". It was one thing having to live with an attic fanatic, but "letting the whole world know" . . . well, that was just too embarrassing for words!

Anyone fortunate enough to delve into the pages of the wonderful history of football will find it a wholly rewarding experience and will, in the process, discover many fascinating stories woven into the fabric of the many facets of the game. Tales of heroes who, from all accounts, could not only walk on water . . . they could dance on it! Of battles won and lost and of Titanic Cup ties which were fought out in burning cauldrons of emotion, before being settled in a blaze of drama.

This book is not my personal attempt to write a history of soccer (many have made a better job of that than I ever could). Nor is it a statistical analysis of the game (figures paint a painful picture of those abysmal performances in the arithmetic class). The motivation to put pen to paper stems, quite simply, from an avid football fan's desire to share just a few of the tales which have gripped his imagination and to remember affectionately men whose exploits thundered across the pages of soccer history and who, though sadly now treated in a diabolical fashion and largely forgotten, should have their names embroidered on golden banners in soccer's "Hall of Fame".

Football does, indeed, weave a rich and colourful tapestry. Much more than just a sport and never merely a hobby, if left unchecked it can touch your life in every way imaginable. One minute plunging the addict into the bottomless pits of despair and, the next, sending him soaring to heights of sheer joy and ecstasy which only those afflicted with as profound an addiction can ever even begin to comprehend. Although gripped by football fever in general and, hopefully, able to appreciate and applaud a player's skills whatever the colour of his jersey, I fell head over heels in love with one club in particular. Way back in the golden days of childhood, when busily rummaging about on those lively and colourful Love Street terracings, I became captivated by the talents of a visiting side which played in green and white and fielded a

"The Famous Five" of Hibernian in their heyday. Left to right . . . Gordon Smith, Bobby Johnstone, Lawrie Reilly, Eddie Turnbull and Wille Ormond.

forward-line which was collectively known as "The Famous Five". Gordon Smith, Bobby Johnstone, Lawrie Reilly, Eddie Turnbull and Willie Ormond . . . the names of those great players tripped off every tongue in the land with ease as they gave the country's top defenders the run-around and sent them spinning in so many directions at once that they must have felt even their blood had been twisted. Like good coffee, they were the perfect blend and the envy of every club in the land.

That fine Hibs side of the 1950s became my religion and, although I adored them all, I worshipped Lawrie Reilly, because he was my god! It is difficult to express adequately just what that fantastic centre-forward meant to me. Nor can I even begin to describe the feelings of inner strength and well-being which he, unknowingly, gave to his diminutive and far-flung disciple. Capped thirty-eight times for Scotland at full international level, Reilly was very much in the superstar category and yet he always seemed to find time to sign an autograph and say a few kind words. I recall confronting him with that grotty

"The Famous Five" plus one pictured in 1979. Left to right . . . Gordon Smith, Bobby Johnstone, Eddie Turnbull, the author, Lawrie Reilly and the late Willie Ormond.

Lawrie Reilly, Hibernian and Scotland.

pencil and requesting his famous signature for the umpteenth time on yet
another grubby piece of paper. Although never a big fella, he seemed like a
towering giant to me. Looking down and patting me on the head, he said,
"Hello son, are you OK?" . . . just a few words were all that was needed and
I have never forgotten that moment.

Today, that once dark hair is as white as freshly fallen snow, but the Reilly
smile is just as broad. Recently I took my ten-year-old son, Robert, to meet
the former hero of Easter Road and Scotland and, needless to say, we were

Wembley, 1953 . . . and England's Alf Ramsay can't prevent Lawrie Reilly from grabbing a last minute equaliser!

made most welcome. Lawrie proudly produced a pile of photographs from his playing days, including a fine action shot of his goal which gave Scotland a very late equaliser in a 2-2 draw versus England at Wembley in 1953 and earned him the nickname of "Last Minute Reilly"; a photograph of the Hibernian side which won the Scottish League Championship by ten clear points in season 1950–51 and countless stills of snapshots which produced many memorable goals for club and country in a success-laden senior playing career which spanned thirteen years. It was a tremendous thrill to meet my boyhood idol again and to appreciate once more that my adulation had not been misplaced and had been devoted not only to a football legend, but, much more importantly, to one of the nicest guys you could ever hope to meet!

Every football fan has a particular hero but, for me, there were two . . . Lawrie Reilly and that fine Hibs, Celtic and Scotland player of the 1960s and 1970s, Pat Stanton. Demonstrating great balance, vision, qualities of leadership and dedication to the game, Stanton was the epitome of the model professional footballer. Capped sixteen times for his country, Pat was deserving of many more honours. He lit up my life as much as any other footballer and is a player whose attributes I will, hopefully, live long enough to describe in graphic and affectionate terms to my grandchildren. When I am far too old and decrepit to dream I will recall with immense pleasure that mine was the wonderful privilege of watching him play on a regular basis:

Pat Stanton with his master's touch,
. . . I watched across the years.
In rain, in wind, in sun and snow,
. . . Wi happiness and tears.
His playing days are over now,
. . . but this much do I know,
When I remember all his skills,
. . . Wi deep content I glow!

My little lad, who's only ten,
He asks me every day:
"Was Stanton really just as great,
My daddy, as you say?"
He was, my boy, I tell you true,
That Paddy was the best.
A giant was he on fitba's stage,
. . . A cut above the rest!

My hero he will always be,
The one whom I'll recall.
Because, you see, I do believe,
He was the best of all.
In years to come, when we're all gone,
They'll still revere his name.
And future men will find Pat's tale,
. . . In soccer's "Hall of Fame"!

Pat Stanton . . . The "King of Easter Road".

Yes . . . every fan has a hero. From the little lad who turns out for the cub football team every Saturday morning, to the old man whose memories of childhood appear all the more rosy in his twilight years and heighten his conviction that the players of today are not even remotely as talented as they were when he was a kid. The marvellous thing is that not even those so-called "experts" can prove any individual's hero-worship to be misplaced . . . can they? It is all very much a matter of opinion . . . isn't it? Heroes come in every shape and size, in all colours and of all creeds. Some are wingers, some full-backs. Some play for Real Madrid, some for Moscow Dynamo. Some wear the red and white of Swindon Town, others the black and gold of East Fife. Some occupy a large corner of the heart forever, while many represent only a fleeting fancy. Evaluation of what constitutes the necessary qualities for a hero is all, my friends, firmly entrenched in the mind and in the eye of the beholder.

Lawrie Reilly "hung up his boots" in 1958 and in that year "yours truly" started to collect football programmes. The hobby was to become almost obsessive with letters, sometimes in pidgin English, being sent all over the world requesting these often elusive bits of paper. Club Secretaries were pestered with pleas for back numbers and many a worthwhile deal was struck in the school playground.

The year 1958 was a momentous one for football. The world of sport mourned when many of Manchester United's "Busby Babes" died in a horrific plane crash at Munich Airport. Bobby Charlton, a young lad who had lived through that terrible air disaster, stunned the 127,874 Hampden crowd when he scored a memorable goal on his first full international appearance at Scotland's national stadium and helped his country to a convincing 4–0 victory over their oldest and deadliest rivals. Despite the fact that their great side had been so tragically decimated, Manchester United bravely reached the FA Cup final and almost everyone in Britain, with the exception of those kindly folk in Bolton, held their breath and prayed that the "Red Devils", with four survivors of the crash in their side, would win the trophy. But Nat Lofthouse, who emerged from the coalface to become England's riproaring centre-forward, clinically and effectively shattered the hopes of a sentimental nation when he scored both the Wanderers' goals in a 2–0 victory. The United dream was in

Bobby Charlton. A memorable goal.

tatters and those Bolton "Trotters" headed north to a heroes' welcome and to place the FA Cup proudly in the Burnden Park trophy room for the fourth time.

Clyde won the Scottish Cup when a deflected Johnny Coyle shot was enough to defeat Hibernian. So the "Bully Wee" gleefully carried that great trophy back to nearby Shawfield for the second time in three years, while the miserable and wretched figure of a little Hibs fan shuffled homewards with a broken heart and tears in his eyes.

In the World Cup finals, a teenage wonder boy called Pele scored twice as those joyous, attack-minded Brazilians cuffed host nation Sweden 5–2 in a classic final played at Stockholm's Solna Stadium.

Yes, 1958 was quite a year on the football front and, over three decades later, I'm still standing on windy, rain-swept terracing with my programme or matchday magazine, as they are sometimes called nowadays, safely enclosed in a polythene bag to protect it from the rigours of the elements.

I know it is hard to comprehend but, believe it or not, there are a few misguided folk who actually admit to having no interest in football whatsoever. Incredible though it may seem, some lost souls would rather go fishing than experience the many and varied thrills to be enjoyed at Partick Thistle's Firhill ground on a match day, while other demented individuals appear to be hooked on afternoon tea and a game of indoor bowling on cold and wet November days, when they could be paying a visit to Recreation Park in Alloa and, apart from enjoying the high standard of football on offer, be partaking in the added pleasure of getting stuck into a pie and Bovril at half-time. Just how can some nutcases possibly prefer bird-watching to Berwick Rangers, hang-gliding to Hamilton Accies, or train spotting to Tranmere Rovers? Oh well, it's a funny old world and I suppose there's room for all kinds!

With the benefit of hindsight, perhaps my father was right and, in a conventional sense, football did wreck my life. But it's been a fine romance and I've certainly got no regrets. Sorry, dad! I don't suppose I achieved the kind of goals which you so fervently hoped I would but, to be honest, your little lad never really wanted to be a brain surgeon anyway!

2

BUT THAT WAS YESTERDAY . . .
AND YESTERDAY'S GONE!

Nobody has the foggiest idea when football was first played. It could have started with some hairy-faced British cave-dweller booting a stone in a gesture of frustration at his inability to spear some fortunate animal. Or, perhaps, it originates from Ivan the Terrible's savage side-kicks hoofing the heads of defeated foes between the animal-skin tents in their encampment. It is just as probable that the navvies who built the Parthenon in Athens between 447 and 438 BC, played some kind of football in their dinner hour, as that the workers in what's left of our Glasgow, Tyneside, or Belfast shipyards, spend their precious lunchbreak belting a ball around within the shadow of the towering cranes until the works' hooter summons those Kenny Dalglish, Jackie Milburn and George Best prototypes back to their labours.

We Britons like to think that organised football originated in these lovely islands of ours but would, maybe, and with a certain amount of reluctance, accept the possibility that the game's roots could lie within the borders of some other country to be found within the continent of Europe. However, the late H.A. Giles of Cambridge University proved conclusively, through his research, that the game was played in China long before Julius Caesar's Roman legions were reputed to have sown the first seeds of the game within these shores. Chinese documents (not the *Topical Times Football Annual*) attribute the origins of football to an Emperor of around 3,000 years BC. (The last time Hibernian won the Scottish Cup?) However, clearer evidence pin-points the beginnings of the game to the third and fourth centuries BC when it formed part of military training, evidence of which is substantiated by a military text book dating from the Han dynasty some 2,000 years ago.

There is indeed a wafer-thin dividing line between fact and fiction when one attempts to disperse those dense and swirling mists of ages in an effort to establish football's precise kick-off time. But, wherever the game emanated from, one fact is absolutely beyond question . . . throughout the Middle Ages the kings and queens of both Scotland and England did everything within their awesome power to suppress the growth of the sport's popularity!

On 13 April 1314, Edward II of England banned the playing of football altogether, "owing to the evil that might arise through many people hustling together". The significance of the year 1314 has not gone unnoticed because, as every self-respecting Scottish schooboy surely knows, that was the year in which King Robert the Bruce and his Scottish army inflicted a humiliating defeat on Edward's English troops at the Battle of Bannock- burn. It is hard to imagine what Edward would have made of the twentieth-century "Tartan Army", with its banners proudly proclaiming "Remember 1314" and recalling Bruce's famous victory over Edward' men. What he and his war-mongering dad, Edward I, who was known as "The Hammer of the Scots" (the 14th- century version of Jimmy Hill), would have thought of vast armies of tartan-clad Scotsmen heading across the border in gigantic, metal flying birds, or hurtling along on huge, snake-like machines which move at great speed on rails, is really only fit for conjecture. Those kings could never have imagined that the crude and unruly game which they detested and tried so hard to abolish would, one day, attain considerable status, become refined and regulated and attract great hordes of invading and marauding Scots to within the very gates of their beloved capital city of London. That there, in front of 100,000 people, the English would be vanquished once again and be forced to capitulate

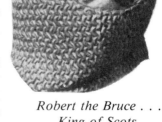

Robert the Bruce . . .
King of Scots.

to just eleven of King Robert's descendants, while legions of weirdly attired and deliriously happy "Jocks" celebrated by dancing *on* and tearing great

Wembley 1977 . . . and rock star, Rod Stewart, gets "carried away" by a section of
that "Tartan Army".

This tartan "Spiderman"
would have terrified Edward's troops . . .

. . . and so would this fire-smoking demon!

lumps of turf *from*, the lush green grass of a huge amphitheatre called Wembley. Neither the bold Edward I nor that much less courageous son of his would have even considered "crossing swords" with the Scots had they been afforded the opportunity of casting their regal eyes over fearsome Scottish "demons" like Spiderman and the fire-smoking monster (above) . . . their very appearance would have scared the living daylights out of their royal personages and sent even the bravest of the English armies retreating in total disarray, not to mention absolute terror!

On 12 June 1349, Edward II also enacted a law against football and similar "foolish games", the warlike king being concerned that the young men of the time were spending too many precious hours kicking a bladder instead of preparing for war by practising archery. Richard II, in 1389, Henry IV, Henry VIII and Elizabeth I, all passed legislation prohibiting the playing of football. However, it has to be admitted that the Scottish kings were no less vociferous in their condemnation of the many rough and varied forms of the "sport".

James III tried to ban the game in 1458, ordering it to be "utterly put down". The anti-football lobby was scathing in its criticism. One critic was Sir Thomas Elyot who, in 1531, said that football was nothing but "beastlie furie and extreme violence, whereof procedeth hurte and consequently rancour, and malice do remaine with them that be wounded; wherefore it is to be put in perpetuall silence". Phillip Stubbes, in his *Anatomie of Abuses* (1583), described football in this way: "I protest unto you it may rather be called a freendly kinde of fighte then a play or recreation, a bloody and murthering practise then a felowly sporte or pastime."

In 1579, in Durham, an unfortunate fellow who answered to the name of John Wonkell was jailed for a week and ordered to do penance in church for being daft enough to get caught playing the game on a Sunday. And, four years later, in 1583, the end of the world was predicted on the grounds that "football and other devilish pastimes were played on the Sabbath, causing necks, legs, backs and arms to be broken, eyes to start out and noses to gush with blood". When you really come to think about it, over 400 years later, things haven't really changed all that much after all, have they?

During the reign of Henry VII, in February 1535, a certain George Taylor was tried and imprisoned for treason. He was accused of saying: "The King is but a knave and liveth in adultery, and is an heretic and liveth not after the laws of God," and further: "I set not by the King's crown, and, if I had it here, I would play at football with it." Taylor denied having made the remarks, and said that if he did say them, he was drunk at the time.

Despite strenuous efforts by those mad monarchs and equally ignorant city fathers to crush the "sport", mob "football", in one crude form or another, flourished over the centuries thanks to the ordinary folk. "The game of football," according to the enlightened and intelligent Montague Sherman in his *Football History* (Badminton Library), "is undoubtedly the oldest of all the English national sports. For at least six centuries the people have loved the rush and struggle of the rude and manly game, and kings with their edicts, divines with their sermons, scholars with their cultured scorn, and wits with their ridicule, have failed to keep the people away from the pastime they enjoyed."

Samuel Pepys in his famous *Diary* describes how, in the great frost of January 1665, "the streets were full of footballs", and it is known that the Lord Protector, Oliver Cromwell, played the game while a student at Sidney Sussex College, Cambridge. One of Cromwell's football recollections is contained in an intriguing letter written by a certain Rev. Cotton Mather, DD, and sent to a Mr George Vaughan on 3 January 1700:

I have heard that when he (*the Rev. John Wheelwright*) was a young spark at the university, he was noted for a more than ordinary stroke at wrestling, and that afterwards, waiting on Cromwell, with whom he had been a contemporary, Cromwell declared unto the gentlemen about him, that he could remember the times he had been more afraid of meeting this gentlemen at football than of anything else since in the field, as he was infallibly sure of being tripped up by him.

OLIVER CROMWELL by Sir Peter Lely . . . painted in accordance with instructions "Not to flatter me at all".

After the death of Cromwell in 1658 and following the Restoration in 1660, King Charles II gave his blessing to the "People's Sport" to the extent that he was a spectator at a match played in 1681 between his servants and those

of the Duke of Albemarle. The monarch is said to have enjoyed the spectacle and to have openly expressed his enthusiasm for the game.

Within the volumes of *Association Football and the Men Who Made It* (published in 1905) we are told that, nearly two centuries later in 1815, one of Scotland's greatest literary sons, Sir Walter Scott, Sheriff of Ettrick Forest, supported his men in a football match against the Earl of Home's Yarrow players and that each gentleman wrote a song. Sir Walter says in his *Lay of the Last Minstrel*:

Some drive the jolly bowl about
With dice and draughts some close the day,
And some with many a merry shout,
Pursue the football play.

That match in 1815, which was a crude mixture of rugby and football and involved hundreds of players, is famous for the description of it by the author of the *Waverley* novels, who wrote:

The appearance of the various parties, marching from their different glens to the place of rendezvous, with pipes playing and loud acclamations, carried back the coldest imagination to the old times when the Foresters assembled with a less peaceable purpose of invading the English territory or defending their own.

There is no indication as to who the respective managers were, or whether or not an official souvenir programme was published as a memento of the occasion. But a "match report" of the time casts some light on the proceedings;

Sir Walter Scott.
Reproduced with the kind permission of Patricia Maxwell Scott.

Master Walter Scott (*the younger*), of Abbotsford, at that time a boy of thirteen, rode around the field waving the old Buccleuch banner, after which the Duke of Buccleuch himself threw up the ball, and the struggle began. Amongst the heaving mass two Selkirk men were to be seen. One of them eventually got the ball and threw it to the other who, not being so much in the thick of the fight, ran off as hard as he could towards the woods of Bow Hill, intending, albeit by a long circuit, to reach the Yarrow goal, and thus bring victory to his side. He would doubtless have succeeded had not a horseman run him down; and so keen was the excitement that the mounted man had some difficulty in getting away from the infuriated players; indeed, Lord Home said he would have shot the rider if a gun had been handy; the match was a tie, no goal being scored on either side.

In Scott's *Lay of the Last Minstrel*, the writer refers to football once again when describing English and Scottish soldiers enjoying "the merry football play" while the protagonists had laid down their weapons for a few hours on the eve of yet another battle. Then we have Sir Walter's advice in verse:

> Then strip, lads, and to it, though sharp be the weather,
> And if, by mischance, you should happen to fall,
> There are worse things in life than a tumble in heather,
> And life is itself but a game at football.

Hear, hear, Sir Walter! But my dear wife simply wouldn't echo these admirable sentiments. She deeply regrets the fact that those uncivilised monarchs in the Middle Ages were unsuccessful in their efforts to show football the red card and to suspend the sport permanently.

Many womenfolk, my much better half included, view the start of each football season with profound apprehension. Those poor, downtrodden, female members of the species envisage yet another long winter when they are deserted on Saturdays as their husbands and boyfriends travel to and from cities like Glasgow and Aberdeen and towns such as Arbroath and Stranraer or Carlisle and Plymouth, either to play the game or to feverishly follow the fortunes of their favourite team. If truth be known, we inconsiderate lads give little or no thought to the wife or girlfriend when we drop in for a quick pint on the way back from our latest football venture. While we're reliving and analysing the game's every move as well as enjoying a pleasant chat, amid peels of laughter, our thoughts seldom stray to the contrasting situation back home:

> Where sits our sulky, sullen dame,
> Gathering her brows like gathering storm,
> Nursing her wrath to keep it warm.

Yes . . . Scotland's national bard, Robert Burns, described the scenario perfectly in his immortal *Tam o' Shanter*.

Although the vast crowds which regularly packed the terracings in the Thirties, Forties and Fifties are a thing of the past, the game is still very much alive. Despite the utterings of total pessimists and derisive comments from people whose attitude to football is not dissimilar to that of Edward II and his henchmen, the game is here to stay. It occupies, has always occupied, and forever will occupy a unique place in the hearts and minds of our people. An integral part of our folklore and traditions and even a key component in the make-up of society, football is no respecter of rank, because, unlike some other sports which I could mention, its kingdom is universal and embraces all of our people. In real terms the wee laddie who kicks an empty lager can around the derelict back streets of our inner cities holds as many shares in football's stock market as the Secretary of the Scottish Football Association or the President of the Football League. Those men who operate at the helm of our clubs and football associations and who circulate in the game's highest echelons, are no more than custodians of a sport which belongs to each and every one of us. Even a cat, they say, can look at a king. Likewise, the penniless little nipper who sneaks under the turnstile or scales the terracing wall has as much right to free admission to our football grounds as the wealthy guests of the game's governing bodies, who arrive at our national stadiums in flashy limousines, accompanied by their uninterested, fur-coated wives, only to be wined and dined and escorted to those cushioned seats in the centre stand.

I simply adore the photograph (overleaf) which, to me, clearly illustrates just what the most popular global game is all about. What marvellous contrasts . . . Pele, arguably football's greatest ever player, emerges from a hut at the Troon Juniors' ground in Ayrshire to be greeted by a real mixed bunch of football fans. The lady sporting a headscarf and standing on a fish box smelling of herring or mackerel which has, somehow, found its way from the local harbour. And the little lad, school-bag dangling from his shoulders, who, along with his friends, has doubtless decided that it was well worth dodging school to catch a glimpse of the great man and, hopefully, manage to obtain the superstar's autograph. The year was 1966 and the Brazilians were training at Troon's Portland Park in preparation for a friendly international versus Scotland at Hampden, which resulted in a 1–1 draw. It's a bit like Frank Sinatra appearing at the Barnsley Miners' Welfare Club, or Dame Margot Fonteyn performing the female lead in the Auchtermuchty Amateur Dance Society's production of *Swan Lake*.

OK . . . so the following quotation has been voiced on more occasions than Bing Crosby's *White Christmas* has been given a spin on record decks and almost as frequently as Terry Wogan's smiling Irish eyes have appeared on the telly. Yes . . . when asked to assess the relevance of football, that

Pele at Troon.

incomparable Scot, the late, great Bill Shankly, came away with what is probably the game's most famous quotation and, in doing so, put the sport firmly into its proper perspective when he replied: "Football is not just a matter of life or death . . . it's much more important than that." Bill Shankly's words were, of course, spoken within the context of his unashamed love of a sport which he perceived as an intrinsically romantic and entertaining game. How horrified "Shanks" would have been had he lived long enough to witness the carnage before the Anfield side's European Cup final appearance against Italian club, Juventus in Belgium's Heysel Stadium on 29 May 1985. It would surely have broken the craggy's Scot's heart to see the name of his beloved club dragged through the gutter and vilified throughout the world thanks to the insanity of a mindless minority.

Although a manifestation of the violent times in which we live, football hooliganism is no new phenomenon and has virtually always been an unwelcome and ugly aspect of the soccer scene. That great Scottish goalkeeper,

Jimmy Brownlie of Third Lanark, who played for his country sixteen times between 1909 and the outbreak of The Great War in 1914, later recalled his personal experiences of two international matches played in Ireland. Although sprinkled with elements of humour, Brownlie's account of the crowd behaviour makes it evident that, on each occasion, the match could have ended in tragic fashion. Having beaten both England and Wales in season 1913–14, Ireland had only to defeat Scotland to win the British International Championship as well as football's version of the "Triple Crown". Belfast was a city in the tight grip of football fever on 14 March 1914 and the Scots were well aware of the fact that a terrific performance was the order of the day if they were to avoid becoming "unstuck" at a Windsor Park venue which, following forty-eight hours of continuous rain, was more like an Irish bog or a Chinese paddy field than an international football pitch. With everything to play for and the score delicately balanced at 0–0, Jimmy Brownlie described a frenzied, and indeed frightening, climax to the match:

Jimmy Brownlie.

Well on in the second half, to the roar of the crowd which packed every available inch of space, Frank Thompson, later to manage Clyde and Ayr, cut in from the left wing and drove a fierce ground shot at me. It squirmed, but I grabbed it again, rose and kicked downfield. It was gathered by our outside-left, Joe Donnachie, who ran on and shot a great goal for Scotland, the leather positively whizzing to the roof of the net. The Irishmen went mad with excitement. They were convinced that Frank's shot had beaten me, that Ireland should have been awarded a goal, and they were further incensed that the picture of what should have been a goal for them was suddenly transformed to one against them.

I prayed for time up to escape the mob. Instead came through the centre in possession the Irish attack leader, Sam Young, Airdrieonians. It wasn't difficult for him to accomplish what he was after . . . score the equaliser. That goal mollified the wild men a bit, but when the final whistle went a few minutes later, and it was realised that the Triple Crown had been denied Ireland, although they had won the championship, pandemonium broke out again. I didn't wait to have a close up of the scene. I did the distance between my goal and the pavilion faster than any champion ped at Powderhall could have done.

Exactly one year earlier, on 15 March 1913, Jimmy Brownlie's previous international appearance in the ''Emerald Isle'' had also been fraught with danger. The venue on this occasion was Dalymount Park in Dublin and the renowned goalkeeper's recollections of the day the fans in the Irish capital went berserk is intriguing, to say the least:

Our left-back that day was Jock (Whitey) Walker, Swindon Town. He was being given a lot of running about by the Irish outside-right, Jimmy Houston, and, on one occasion, Walker's charge on Houston was of the robust type. The Irish on the terracing immediately took an emphatic dislike to Jock, and they let him understand the fact in no uncertain manner. Jock didn't worry, but continued to mak' siccar where Houston was concerned. The crowd became decidedly bad tempered, but it was not until the end of the game that the fun really started.

In those days, at the final whistle, there used to be a scamper by the players to capture the ball as a trophy, or memento of the game. Our outside-left George Robertson, Motherwell and Sheffield Wednesday, had the ball at his feet when the end of the match was signalled, and he at once stooped down and grabbed the leather. One of his opponents knocked it out of his clutch. George regained possession, but once more it was sent flying from his clutch. That was too much for human nature, as represented by George Robertson, who socked the culprit on the jaw. Talk about the results of applying a flaming torch to a bundle of timber soaked in petrol. There was one almighty roar of rage from the crowd, the members of which had arrived at Dalymount, no doubt, ostensibly peace-loving citizens. Now they were howling, screaming Dervishes, clamouring for blood.

Along with the rest of my mates, I had been strolling slowly to the pavilion, but now every one of us seemed imbued with the speed of the antelope. Inside the dressing-room we breathed the sigh of relief born of narrow escape from a hundred forms of death. We had stripped in our hotel, and each of us had only his overcoat with him. It was a good job, for the crowd that had swarmed on to the field shouting murder, now hurled themselves at the dressing-room and smashed in two sides of it. We fled as the rioters rushed in and succeeded in clambering into our two-horse-pulled brake. We were surrounded. Robertson was the man they were after. George, however, wasn't in the brake. He had succeeded in concealing himself somewhere in the half-wrecked pavilion where he remained for a couple of hours before making his exit in borrowed clothes. When Robertson could not be secured for execution the roar went up for Walker. Jock bent down to hide his face, but he had already been spotted. Somehow or other the mob was prevented from clambering on to the brake by mounted police. We were pelted with apples, oranges, and all sorts of missiles as we made our way to our hotel, heavily guarded by police. At the hotel entrance there was another big crowd and Jock Walker got a bit of a mauling as he struggled to the door. Once we were inside we were safe, although, needless to say, we had two hours' anxiety awaiting for the return of George Robertson.

Scotland's 2–1 victory was clearly inconsequential when viewed in the wider context of events. And, when you read that sort of account of occurrences at a football match, perhaps old Edward II and his cronies weren't quite so stupid after all! But, maybe, even those kings and queens of bygone days would have cast more tolerant regal eyes on football had they been privileged to witness the glittering occasion that is a twentieth century FA or Scottish Cup Final . . . if only to admire the gleaming silverware on display!

Originally costing £56 12s 11d, a price which included a set of medals, the Scottish Cup has enjoyed a very colourful existence since it was first presented to Queen's Park in 1874. What a grand tale that historic old trophy could divulge if only it were able to converse with us. More than just a lump of silver, it has been around since the infancy of the organised game in Scotland and has been the star attraction at Scottish Cup Finals played at Hampden Park and, among other venues, Hamilton Crescent, Kinning Park and Logie Green in Edinburgh.

In contrast, the FA Challenge Cup cannot claim such a lengthy or illustrious pedigree. Its silver first caught the light of day in season 1910–11 and it is the third trophy to be competed for in the English competition. The first FA Cup cost £20, with Queen's Park contributing a guinea and Wanderers beating the Royal Engineers 1–0 in the inaugural final played at Kennington Oval in 1872. Some time between the hours of 9.30 p.m. on Wednesday, 11 September 1895, and 7.30 a.m. on the Thursday morning, the cup was stolen while on display

The Birmingham premises from where the FA Cup was stolen in 1895.

in a football outfitter's in Birmingham and, despite the incentive of a £10 reward, it was never seen again! Aston Villa, the holders, were held responsible and fined £25 by the FA. An exact replica, costing the same as the unfortunate Villa's fine, was struck and, after fifteen years of competition, this second English trophy was withdrawn and presented to Lord Kinnaird on 6 February 1911, in recognition of his services to the game and on his completion of twenty-one years as President of the Football Association. The current FA Cup, purchased for fifty guineas, was made in Bradford and, coincidentally, was first won by Bradford City in 1911. The bill of fare at the Bradford club's celebration dinner surely consisted of Scotch broth and haggis rather than roast beef and Yorkshire pudding . . . because a record eight Scots played for the Bradford Cup-Final side which won the trophy after beating Newcastle United 1–0 in a replay.

Bradford City, FA Cup winners 1911. Players only. Back row left to right: Torrance, O'Rourke, Mellors, McDonald and Devine. Middle: Gildea, Campbell, Spiers, Robinson, Taylor and Thompson. Front: Logan and Bond.

In England folks are understandably and justifiably proud of their trophy and of the annual Wembley Cup Final. But I like to think that our grand old Scottish Cup is very aware of its heritage and brimful of recollections of the exploits of teams like Queen's Park, Vale of Leven, East Fife, Celtic, Rangers and other great sides which it has met along the way. Perhaps the silver trophy does, in its quieter moments, reflect nostalgically on the performances of shining stars like Bobby Walker of Hearts, Celtic's Jimmy Quinn, Bob McPhail of Rangers, Dunfermline Athletic goalkeeper, Eddie Connachan, and countless other football "giants" who have crossed its path, kissed and cuddled it and, over the decades, raised it to their lips to drink gallons of celebratory champagne:

I laugh at all you mortal men,
Your spirits down and up.
But me, I simply sparkle on
. . . Cos I'm the Scottish Cup!
I watch you as you dash about
. . . Your lives so short, you see!
And wonder why you try so hard,
. . . To get your hands on me!

You're daft enough to think you know
. . . A lot about the game,
About the players to be found
. . . In football's "Hall of Fame".
But you can think just what you like,
Because I'm sure, you see,
What you guys know of fitba's tale,
. . . Is nowt compared wi' me!

Your human hearts, they beat so fast,
I watch you get dementit.
But how I love you football lads,
. . . Great friendships we've cementit.
Auld Scotia is a grand wee place
The best o' fitba' nations.
It is wi' pride, I've watched yir skills,
. . . Across those generations!

So when you gaze at me today,
. . . And wonder what I'm thinkin',
Look closely all my mortal pals,
. . . Cos at you, I'll be winkin'.
And if you play our bonnie game
. . . Wi' sporting skill and style,
Perhaps, if you look close enough,
You'll even catch me smile!

FREDERICK
MARTIN·JNR

Football has many faces and, unlike that wise old Scottish Cup, they are not always smiling and good-natured. But it has to be remembered that thousands of matches are played up and down the country each and every week at venues as varied as Villa Park or the village green, and the vast majority are violence free!

Football arouses as much passion in the hearts of twentieth-century man as primitive forms of the sport almost certainly did long before the fall of the Roman Empire, The Battle of Bannockburn, or *The Saint and Greavsie* show . . . and it will continue to do so! Unfortunately many members of the "gutter press" prefer to concentrate on the darker, more sinister side of soccer and derive great pleasure from unearthing and exaggerating a "sensational and exclusive" story concerning the private life of some unfortunate player or manager. Those sick-minded muck-rakers, whose own life style is often ten times more vile and reprehensible than that of the victim, are despicable examples of individuals, some of whom glean a very comfortable living from the game, yet who demonstrate no feelings whatsoever for what football is really all about.

I would rather contemplate the happier face of soccer, because its countenance personifies a sport brimful of romance and filled with the warm glow of nostalgia; an art form, the illustrious story of which is littered with men of artistic genius and which, when compared with any other sport, is still, quite simply, in a league of its own.

However, in recent years and in the opinion of this fan, an over-emphasis on the role and importance of coaching has taken a lot of the entertainment value out of football. It saddens me greatly to watch ten-year-old kids standing shivering in the right or left midfield position on some cold November morning, frightened to stray out of their designated "box" in case they should wreck the pre-match plans which their schoolteacher or boys' club leader has rigidly mapped out. Lads of that age are instinctively attracted to the ball in a manner akin to iron filings rushing to a powerful magnet. It was from within such a huddled mass of tiny bodies, each intent on becoming the sole possessor of the ball or tin can, that legends like Stanley Matthews, George Best and Jimmy Johnstone refined their God-given talents, learned how to caress and control the ball, to jink, swerve and dribble, to mesmerise their young opponents and to emerge from the pack with the object of all that frantic endeavour at their twinkling toes. Within such scenes of gay and unbridled abandon are the seeds of football genius sown.

In the 1930s, in far-off Budapest, a bare-footed Hungarian boy called Ferenc Puskas played with a ball made from his mum's stocking. That skinny lad went on, of course, to become the portly "Galloping Major" of Honved and Hungary fame, before setting Spanish eyes alight with many illuminating performances for the greatest club side ever, Real Madrid. In his book, *Captain of Hungary*, published in 1956, Puskas says: "I will write my life as a footballer as if it were a love story, for who shall say it is not? It began with my great love of football, and it will end in the same way. . . . " Nobody with a coaching certificate buried in his tracksuit pocket taught Puskas how the game should be played!

Ferenc Puskas . . . "The Galloping Major".

Eusebio, that "Black Panther" who starred for Benfica and Portugal in the 1960s, was another example of a natural footballer whose ball skills, positional sense and instinctive eye for goal, owed little or nothing to the mediocre gibberish of the coaching manual. Thank goodness I'm old enough to have seen men like Puskas and Eusebio play, to have, on many occasions, witnessed the magic of George Best and the wonderful, untamed arrogance of that delectable Rangers and Scotland star, Jim Baxter.

Having said all that, it is evident that modern football demands and, indeed, can benefit from, a certain amount of coaching and pre-match planning. Great inspirational managers like Jock Stein and Don Revie proved beyond doubt that the master tactician can motivate and transform a group of previously disorganised players into an effective and successful unit. But it has all gone too far!

Eusebio . . . "The Black Panther".   *Jim Baxter . . .delectable!*

Tommy McInally of Celtic and Scotland fame, who played for six senior clubs between 1919 and 1931, was certainly no advocate of an indulgence in theory when it came to football. A colourful and often controversial character who revelled in periodic confrontations with authority, Tommy was inclined to become more than a little hot under the collar when subjected to the antics of soccer theorists of an earlier football era . . . as he emphasised in the October 1949 edition of *Scottish Football Digest*:

> I recall an incident in my playing days . . . not with Celtic. The manager and directors called a meeting with the players, and we trooped in to see a board laid out as a football pitch with eleven corks positioned after the fashion of a team's line-up. While the players stood around, the directors commenced to move the corks about, giving what they erroneously believed were examples of good positional play. A cork would be moved from inside-right to inside-left, and so on. This ridiculous performance went on for about fifteen minutes, and I could stand it no longer. I kicked the board and the corks into the air, and remarked to the rest of the players, "Come on hame. The other team has scored."

Well done Tommy, well done!

In the March 1956 edition of *Football Monthly*, sportswriter John MacAdam described another incident which gives us an insight into the character of Tommy McInally:

> The great Celt, Tommy McInally, was the man who sat on the ball in a Rangers-Celtic five-a-side final. Tommy played back-and-goal. Celtic were one up and the first time the ball came to Tommy, he sat on it . . . and all the exhortations of the referee and the crowd wouldn't make him get off it. There he sat, like a hen on an egg, certain in the knowledge that none of the five Rangers dare come out of position and leave his colleagues hopelessly outnumbered. There was almost a break-in before they got McInally off his roost.

Tommy McInally.

Dribbling, inside-forward and winger . . . words as quaint and alien to youngsters as farthing, threepenny bit and tramcar, words from a bygone football vocabulary which are evocative of skills straight out of the game's top drawer. . . . but that was yesterday and yesterday's gone!

However, despite the restrictions imposed on the modern player, the game still manages to produce men of magic. Men like England's Glen Hoddle, Argentina's Diego Maradona and Scotland's Davie Cooper. Players with an immense range of individual skills who have not been churned out on football's version of the factory production line and who, thankfully, do not easily adapt to the pre-planned patterns outlined in the coaching manual. To a degree Kenny Dalglish, of Celtic, Liverpool and Scotland fame, comes into this category. I recall watching the future "King Kenny" in the late 1960s when, as a fresh-faced youngster, he was starring with Scottish Junior side,

Kenny Dalglish scoring for Cumbernauld United versus Kirkintilloch Rob Roy in the late 1960s.

Cumbernauld United, and already displaying the controlled ability and goalscoring flair which was to develop into one of football's most exciting post-war talents. Happily, somewhere in the back streets of Derby and Dundee, Swansea and Sunderland, as well as in the poverty-ridden shanty towns which encircle sprawling South American cities like Rio de Janeiro and

Buenos Aires, there are other kids who are simply unable to comprehend or adapt to imposed patterns, and who would shrug their narrow shoulders if asked to fit into a plan. Nippy little football nonconformists from such surroundings, as well as from the ranks of those boys' clubs and school teams, who are the Hoddles, Dalglishes and Maradonas of tomorrow and who will, one day, hold the key to success for their countries in the World Cups of 1998 and beyond. By then they will be men on whose broad shoulders will fall the considerable responsibility of projecting the true skills of this enthralling game into the twenty-first century. Theirs will be the Herculean task of exorcising the ghosts of past masters and of disproving the widely-held conviction that almost all the truly great legends of soccer are to be found locked away within the pages of football history.

In 1892, while the Prince of Wales, the future King Edward VII, became Patron of the Football Association and continued that patronage on his accession to the throne, the animosity which most of the sovereigns of earlier times had shown towards this greatest of games now became a thing of the past. Royalty had finally, if somewhat belatedly, come to accept the elevated status which football had attained in the hearts and minds of the people, as well as within the life of the nation. On 3 April 1909, the Prince of Wales (George V) watched England beat Scotland 2–0 at the Crystal Palace and, five years

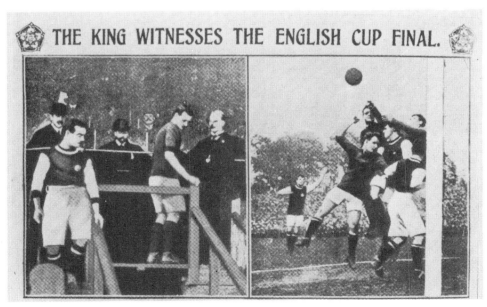

King George V at the 1914 FA Cup final.

later, on 25 April 1914, the last FA Cup Final played at the old Crystal Palace was an historic occasion worthy of a chapter in any definitive story of football because on that day King George V became the first reigning monarch to attend an FA Cup Final. It was Burnley and Liverpool who emerged as finalists from a record entry of 476 clubs and neither of those famous names had previously appeared in an FA Cup Final. After a dour struggle, Burnley won 1–0 with centre-half Boyle becoming the first Cup-winning captain to receive the trophy from royal hands.

Since that day in 1914, members of the Royal Family have been present at many of football's glamour occasions and the monarchy and the "People's Game" appear to enjoy a fairly harmonious relationship. But I, for one, still get the feeling that their Royal Highnesses are not entirely at ease with the sport, that they feel infinitely more at home seated in the Royal Box at a Twickenham rugby international, at a Wimbledon tennis final, or a Lords Test match, or Royal Ascot. . . . but maybe I've got hold of the wrong end of the shooting-stick!

King George VI, D. Bowie (President of the SFA), Princess Elizabeth (now Queen Elizabeth II), and Field-Marshal Viscount Montgomery at an England v Scotland match in 1944.

In this ancient and historic land of ours success on the football field out-shines any other area of achievement. Why then, I ask myself, with my tongue only slightly tucked in my cheek, are statues not erected in cities throughout the UK to honour the "giants" of football? How fitting it would be if the peerless Alex James, who set London alight with his glorious performances for Arsenal in the halcyon days of the 1930s, shared a place of honour along-side Lord Nelson in the capital's Trafalgar Square. If monuments can be erected up and down the land honouring and recognising the achievements of writers, politicians, soldiers and sailors, why shouldn't a statue of George Best, for example, be placed on a pedestal high above Belfast's Royal Avenue? He is, after all, that city's most famous son! Likewise erect one of that Welsh wizard, Ivor Allchurch, in Swansea, Bobby Charlton in Ashington and Sir Matt Busby in his native Bellshill. Surely those great Hearts and Scotland inside-forwards, Bobby and Tommy Walker, are worthy of inclusion among the many statues to be found in the vicinity of Edinburgh's Princes Street? Naturally, any monument to these two famous players would have to be sited at the West End of Britain's most beautiful thoroughfare, as near as possible to the scene of their many triumphs in the Hearts' ground at Tynecastle. But what about the East End of Princes Street? Well, the prime site there is currently occupied by the monument to Sir Walter Scott, a gifted writer who was clearly a man ahead of his time, not least, as already mentioned, in his appreciation of the skills and finer points of football. Appropriate, therefore, that this great man is seated in his monument in closer proximity to Easter Road stadium, the home of Hibernian Football Club! I make that claim with just the hint of a mischievous twinkle in my eye and in the knowledge that Hearts' name originates from Scott's novel *Tales of my Landlord, Second Series (The Heart of Midlothian)*, which the author wrote in 1818. Indeed, it was the same Sir Walter Scott who expressed his affection for the great game in the lines:

> And when it is over we'll drink a blithe measure,
> To each laird and each lady that witnessed our fun.
> And to every blithe heart that took part in our pleasure
> To the lads that have lost and to the lads that have won.

Somehow we have managed to complicate what is, in essence, a simple game. Winning is far too important nowadays, with not nearly enough importance being placed on the manner in which victory is achieved—a fact sickeningly highlighted by the attitude of a present-day coach who said: "Better to win a scrappy and dull game 1–0, than to open the play up, place the emphasis on attack and lose 5–4." What utter rubbish!

No respecter of football coaches in the first place, the enigmatic, yet brilliant, Tommy McInally would have turned purple with rage on hearing that kind of nonsensical approach to the sport. "Football games should be played on the field . . . not in flights of imagination," Tommy once said. "I believe in coaching, but I believe that true coaching, as far as the adult is concerned, can only be had on the field of play . . . by playing alongside the better and more experienced player."

It is, perhaps, just as well that you are no longer with us, Tommy, because I don't think that you would be over-enthusiastic about the way in which football has developed since your day. Coaching is the key word in the modern game and it can be difficult to scale the soccer success ladder if you are not in possession of a coaching certificate.

A great football enthusiast, Scotland's national coach, Andy Roxburgh, is likeable, highly talented and passionately committed to his task. But his official title of Technical Director leaves me stone cold. Technical Director!

Andy Roxburgh . . . Scottish international football's Technical Director!

Isn't that a dreadful misnomer for someone in charge of football, Tommy? Titles such as that are well suited for the boss of an urban renewal project or the head of a computer research operation . . . but they should find no place whatsoever in the vocabulary of football.

A vast army of coaches now employ the most modern technology at their disposal to control and manipulate players in a manner which would have been both impossible and unacceptable when you were playing, Tommy. The game is being choked to death by tacticians. Thank God there are still a few rebels around who are prepared to kick the corks in the air and to fire a broadside at those numerous theorists. "Boot Out The Coaches" . . . that was the

Willie Morgan.

opinion voiced by former Burnley, Manchester United and Scotland player, Willie Morgan, in a *Daily Express* headline on 15 June 1988. A highly talented winger, who was capped twenty-one times between 1968 and 1974, Morgan was uncompromising in his condemnation of the coaching lobby. "The coaches have ruined the game because they want robots and hate to see quality players who can think for themselves," said Morgan, adding: "The great teams had flair and they had managers like Jock Stein, Matt Busby, Brian Clough, Bill Shankly, Bill Nicholson and now Kenny Dalglish at Liverpool. None of these were coaches. Look at any great team and you will see a manager in charge of them rather than a coach. Coaches need to be pushed into the background to let the kids come through." Am I right in assuming that you would echo those sentiments, Tommy?

This obsessive over-emphasis on the importance of coaching has, alas, spread like a cancer through all levels of the sport. I was deeply saddened when my son, Robert, then eight years old, came home from playing for his boys' club and told me that he had been scolded for scoring a goal when he wasn't supposed to be in a forward position. "Scoring goals is the most important thing in football, isn't it, Dad?" said the little mite. Telling him to ignore the blackboard boffins, to enjoy the game and to score as many goals as he could, I patted him on the head and off he went with an air of reassurance and a glint in his eye. Kids of that age believe everything that their dads tell them, don't they? I can only hope that, one fine day, little Robert will become as talented and worldly-wise as the marvellous Willie Morgan.

However, despite the absurdities and complexities of the modern game, football remains for legions of devotees nothing short of a religion, with those players assuming god-like status and the stadiums becoming the places of worship. Adored and revered as much as any player in the history of the sport, Sir Stanley Matthews has deservedly enjoyed the adulation of millions. In October 1987 the greatest accolade possible was conferred on "The Wizard of the Dribble" when a statue of Stanley Matthews was unveiled in Stoke.

Sir Stanley Matthews at the unveiling of his statue.

At last, an enduring monument to a footballer and overdue recognition that the talents of players such as Stanley Matthews are, in their own way, every bit as significant and praiseworthy as the achievements of men such as Byron, Shakespeare and Wordsworth. I, for one, fervently hope that the Matthews statue is the first of many.

That talented former Clyde and Scotland left-back, Harry Haddock, appreciates more than most why Stan is deserving of such an honour, because Matthews roasted the popular Clyde man when England crushed the Scots 7–2 at Wembley in 1955. To Harry's eternal credit he never resorted to unfair tactics and was universally applauded for his sporting attitude. What Harry didn't know then was that the meticulous Matthews, on hearing that Haddock had a fair turn of speed, had fasted for almost a week in preparation for his joust with the Clyde and Scotland defender.

Two or three years ago, when in the company of Harry and his Clyde and Scotland team-mate, Tommy Ring, Tommy asked me if I knew what Matthews' favourite breakfast was. Wondering just what this incurable joker was talking about, I told him that I had no idea, at which point he said: "It was Haddock on toast" . . . and Harry, well used to Tommy's sense of humour, simply smiled.

I wonder if old Oliver Cromwell was right- or left-footed? Do there exist any faded parchments resembling match programmes which date back to those dark days in the Middle Ages? . . . somehow I doubt it! But, whichever way you look at it, Sir Walter Scott certainly hit the nail very firmly on the head when he wrote: "Life is itself but a game at football."

Harry Haddock . . .
had a fair turn of speed.

3

UNDERNEATH THE ARCHES

Steve Bloomer, Alex James, John Charles, George Best, Denis Law . . . yes indeed, the history of British international football is bejewelled with the names of star players who, through wearing their country's colours with distinction, have become immortalised in the annals of our national game. Football in Great Britain has long been associated with what has been called the "working class" and, understandably, many believe that the "Beautiful Game", as the great Pele so accurately and affectionately calls it, owes its modern origin solely to the areas of urban depravation and to the less affluent sectors of society. It is generally felt that it was lads from mining villages in traditional counties like Ayrshire and Northumberland, boys from the squalor of nineteenth-century cities like Glasgow and Liverpool as well as kids from the back streets of Belfast, who nurtured the sport and laid the foundations of the game as we know it today. It is, therefore, hard to believe that the "People's Game" was, for many years, a favourite pastime of public schoolboys and that it was, in fact, within bastions of privilege like Eton and Harrow that the organised game's greatest strengths lay.

Quintin Hogg, W.H. Gladstone MP and The Honourable Arthur Fitzgerald Kinnaird . . . what connection, you ask, could they possibly have with Scottish international football? In fact, all three of those eminent Victorian gentlemen played for "Scotland" and were closely linked with the establishment of the Scotland versus England international series.

The only son of the tenth Baron Kinnaird of Rossie Priory, Inchtore, Perthshire, The Honourable Arthur Fitzgerald Kinnaird was an all-round sportsman who represented Cambridge at fives, tennis and swimming and, in 1867, won an international canoe race at the Paris Exhibition. Kinnaird could play in any position on the football field and throughout his eventful life the man's talents shone in many different spheres of activity. During his footballing days with the Old Etonians and the Wanderers he won five FA Cup winner's medals and was a member of the Scottish side beaten 4–2 by England at Kennington Oval in 1873, in the first full international match staged south of the border. With his splendid red beard, long, white-flannel trousers, jersey and quartered cap, from all accounts Kinnaird was an impressive figure of a man during his playing days.

His on-field exertions over, Arthur Kinnaird, who succeeded to the barony in 1887, went on to become not only a member of the House of Lords, but a Lord High Commissioner of the Church of Scotland, President of the

Lord Kinnaird.

YMCA of England and President of the Football Association for a remarkable thirty-three years. Those members of the House of Lords who sat in that glittering, gilded chamber, resplendent in coronets and ermine and whose sporting interests were largely confined to the polo field or the grouse moor just didn't know what to make of their football-daft Lord. But due to the endless support which Lord Kinnaird gave to the game he loved, as well as his efforts to improve the welfare of the poorer sections of the community, he enjoyed the genuine affection of the masses of the population. ''I believe,'' Kinnaird once said when referring to football, ''that all right minded people have good reason to thank God for the great progress of this popular national game.''

That colourful British political figure and former Lord Chancellor, The Right Honourable Lord Hailsham of St Marylebone (formerly Quintin Hogg), is very proud of his Scottish descent and of his grandfather's achievements both in the community and on the football field. In response to a letter enquiring into Quintin Hogg's connection with the sport, Lord Hailsham informed me that his "grandfather was the captain of Old Etonian FC for seven years, during which time the club never sustained a defeat and captained the first seven Scots teams against England in the years 1864–1870. In addition to his prowess as a footballer, he also played cricket and fives and was a keen cyclist."

Lord Hailsham of St Marylebone.   *Quintin Hogg (1845–1903).*

In the 1860s international matches of a very unofficial nature were arranged by well-heeled former pupils of English public schools and universities and the teams were made up of "old boys" from institutions like the aforementioned Eton and Harrow. Proof of Scottish blood in the veins, however much diluted, was deemed sufficient eligibility to play in the Scottish side. By 1870 the Football Association was in on the act and, from November of that year until February 1872, four matches were played under the auspices of that organisation. C.W. Alcock, Secretary of the FA, wrote to the *Glasgow Herald* on 3 November 1870 asking for nominations for a Scottish team. It was generally felt that there would be a wholly negative response from north of the border, but Queen's Park thought differently and nominated Robert Smith, a member of a famous Queen's Park family based in London. FA Secretary Alcock selected both teams for a match which England won 1–0 on 19 November 1870.

Of the four matches played, and which are now regarded as unofficial, the best Scotland could achieve was a 1–1 draw in a game which took place at Kennington Oval in London on 28 February 1871. The Honourable A.F.Kinnaird kept goal for the Scots, while William H. Gladstone MP (son of British Prime Minister, William Ewart Gladstone) and Quintin Hogg formed part of the Scottish defensive set-up. Scotland won the toss and, ably assisted by a strong wind, took the lead after fifteen minutes when C.E. Nepean of University College Oxford scored. From all accounts, this reverse brought England back to life and, according to a newspaper report of the time, "For upwards of half an hour the efforts of the English forwards were frustrated by the faultless kicking of Hogg and Gladstone." Eventually R.S.F.Walker equalised for England, C.W. Alcock, Secretary of the FA, being involved in the successful build-up to the goal.

Arthur Kinnaird won the first of those five FA Cup winner's medals when he played in the Wanderers side which beat Oxford University 2–0 in the 1872–73 final. Three years later Kinnaird and Quintin Hogg were team-mates in an Old Etonians side which opposed the Wanderers at The Oval in the 1875–76 FA Cup Final and, on this occasion, Hogg kept goal while Kinnaird occupied one of the defensive berths. The teams were level at the interval and, although the Old Etonians had the better of the second-half, they were unable to take advantage of their superiority. They did, however, think that they had won the trophy when, following a corner-kick, the ball appeared to be driven between the Wanderers' goalposts. Unfortunately the woodwork collapsed on impact and so the referee was unable to award a goal and the game ended 0–0. The cup had tantalisingly slipped from Old Etonians' grasp when they had looked set to triumph. But even greater anguish lay ahead of Kinnaird and

Hogg because a week later at the same venue Wanderers won 3–0 in a replay to record the first of three successive FA Cup Final victories.

Interestingly, Kinnaird switched his allegiance yet again and played in the Wanderers' goal when they beat Oxford University 2–0 in the 1876–77 final and in the half-back line when the Royal Engineers were beaten 3–1 in the 1877–78 final. Where was Kinnaird the following year? The answer is back in an Old Etonians Cup Final side which beat Clapham Rovers 1–0 at the Oval. Kinnaird was presented with his fifth winner's medal when Old Etonians beat Blackburn Rovers 1–0 in the 1881–82 final . . . the eighth of an amazing *nine* Cup Final appearances!

Born into this world on St Valentine's Day 1845, Quintin Hogg (grandfather of the present Lord Hailsham) was the fourteenth of sixteen children for Sir James Weir Hogg and Lady Hogg. Despite the number of offspring, his was a very wealthy and privileged family and during his early years Quintin knew nothing of the contrasting poverty and suffering endured by masses of the population in places like London's East End. When "Piggy", as his friends affectionately called him, first witnessed this terrible poverty as a young man in his late teens, he was overwhelmed with pity for the "poor little beggars" who crossed his path. In fact, the plight of the deprived in London so haunted Quintin Hogg that he pledged himself to do all within his power to help them. The man may have been born with the proverbial silver spoon in his mouth, but Hogg was no gentleman of leisure. Quintin was to spend the rest of his days in almost constant devotion to others.

Throughout his childhood, Hogg's father had spared no expense in ensuring that the boy received the best possible education. Sir James had many commercial interests and had earmarked his youngest son for a business career in London which, although a vibrant and bustling place in the early Victorian Age, was also a city scarred by terrible slums and riddled with cesspools of vice and corruption.

On leaving Eton at Christmas 1863, Quintin did indeed embark on a business career in London and it was there that he first encountered the horrific deprivation which vast numbers of the capital's inhabitants were forced to endure. One day, when strolling nonchalantly in Trafalgar Square while the church bells were ringing, Quintin happened to stumble across two little paupers. "What do you know about God?" he enquired. "He's the one wot sends us to 'ell," came the prompt reply . . . a response which astonished Hogg and was to leave a lasting impression on the mind of the deeply religious young man.

By the mid-1860s those Old Etonian footballing friends, Quintin Hogg and Arthur Kinnaird, had rented a sparsely furnished, candlelit room in "Of

Alley'' (later York Place) for the princely sum of £12 a year. Due to the fact that these seedy premises were crawling with rats and mice, Hogg and Kinnaird spent many a night sleeping in hammocks in that vermin-ridden room. And it was in those primitive, squalid and almost Spartan surroundings that Quintin started his ''Ragged School'' for boys . . . the aim being to provide a broad industrial education for as many as possible of the poor little urchins who aimlessly roamed the streets of London. By day Hogg was a successful businessman with many varied connections in the worlds of trade and commerce and by night he earned extra money for the waifs and strays whom he had committed himself to help, by holding horses, blacking boots and doing odd jobs. Quintin's father was totally unaware that on two or three evenings a week his son ate pigs' trotters or tripe and onions purchased from a barrow and spent the night curled up in a barrel covered with tarpaulin or on a ledge underneath the Adelphi Arches, in an attempt to gain first-hand experience of just what destitution meant to the individual in the cruel and heartless streets of London. ''I felt,'' said Hogg, ''as though I should go mad unless I did something to try and help some of the wretched little chaps I used to see running about the streets.'' The following is Quintin's own account of his earliest attempt to come to their aid:

The House in ''Of Alley'', afterwards known as York Place,
in which Mr. Hogg began his Ragged School work.

My first effort was to get a couple of crossing-sweepers whom I picked up near Trafalgar Square, and offered to teach them how to read. In those days the Thames Embankment did not exist and the Adelphi Arches were open to both the tide and the street. With an empty beer bottle for a candlestick and a tallow candle for illumination, two crossing-sweepers as pupils, your humble servant as teacher, and a couple of Bibles as reading books, what grew into the Polytechnic was practically started. We had not been engaged in our reading very long when, at the far end of the arch, I noticed a twinkling. "Kool ecilop," shouted one of the boys, at the same moment "doucing the glim" and bolting with his companion, leaving me in the dark with my upset beer bottle and my douced candle, forming a spectacle which seemed to arouse suspicion on the part of our friend the policeman, whose light it was that had appeared in the distance. However, after scrutinizing me for some time by the light of his bulls-eye, he moved on, leaving me in a state of mental perturbation as to what the mystic words I had heard hollered out meant, and to ask myself what I, who a year before had been at Eton, was doing at that time of night under an Adelphi Arch? Afterwards, when I became proficient in back slang, I knew that "kool ecilop" was "look out for the police" spelt backwards, the last word being evidently the original of the contraction "slop", a familiar nick-name for the police of London today. Altogether I did not think my first essay a very successful one, and I cast about in my mind how I could learn the language of those boys, and ascertain their real wants and their ways of life.

Although the young footballing philanthropist came to be regarded as a knight in shining armour by the unfortunates whom he helped in the London which Charles Dickens knew so well, he also had the reputation of being a determined enemy of crime and, consequently, was subjected to constant danger in the streets which Dickens portrayed so graphically in *Oliver Twist*. In a letter Quintin described a lucky escape to one of his sisters:

I nearly got potted the other night. I was humbugged into a room to buy photos, and they did their best to shoot and stab me. I only succeeded in getting off by a determined resistance and the bursting of a shutter, the bar of which fortunately came down, shutter and all, when I wrenched at it in desperation.

Despite the obvious risks, Hogg's determination to champion the cause of London's poor was absorbing more and more of his time. He started English classes for many of the flower girls of Charing Cross and like Professor Higgins, who had his hands full attempting to educate Elisa Doolittle in the marvellous musical *My Fair Lady*, Quintin required a great deal of patience to enable him to stick to what must have proved a daunting task. During daylight hours, when engaged in the machinations of the business world or playing for Old Etonians and "Scotland", an army of his boys were busily shining shoes all over Central London and earning much-needed cash for the ever growing "Ragged School".

By the 1870s Hogg's friend, Arthur Kinnaird, had become something of a national hero thanks to his exploits on the football field. On one occasion adoring fans took the horses out of the shafts of his carriage and pulled the great man and his party the last few hundred yards to the Oval pavilion for a Cup Final. When Kinnaird wasn't playing football or, as he once did, entertaining a Cup final crowd by standing on his head in front of the grandstand, he always managed to find some time to lend his support to Hogg's crusade on behalf of London's destitute.

By now Quintin Hogg's family was fully aware of his activities and, although his father outwardly disapproved, he secretly admired his son's work. However, Quintin incurred the full might of Sir James's wrath when, on one occasion, he borrowed his father's carriage, filled it with street urchins and took them for a ride in fashionable Hyde Park.

Every adventure which Quintin embarked on was tackled with enthusiasm and total commitment. Just as he had played so whole-heartedly for those "old boys" who represented "Scotland" when international football was little more than an embryo, so too did he give his all for the infant "Ragged School" which he had founded and which, in 1882, he was so gratified to see grow into the London Polytechnic. Quintin was a man who put his money where his mouth was or, more accurately, where his heart was, donating the then, and still, staggering sum of over £100,000 from his personal fortune to the cause of helping the destitute in London.

The Victorian Age was an era of enormous change and significant innovation. Queen Victoria came to the throne in 1837 and before she died in 1901 Britain's longest-reigning monarch witnessed the discovery of such inventions as the motor car, wireless, telephone and electric light. It probably escaped the Queen's notice but S.W.Widdowson, the famous Notts Forest and England player, brought out and registered shin-guards in 1874, while a certain Mr Brodie from Liverpool invented and patented goalnets which were first used in the North versus South match in January 1891. It is just conceivable that life would be tolerable minus luxuries such as the electric light and the telephone . . . but just where would we all be without shin-guards and goalnets?

Rightly proud of their wide-ranging pioneering skills, those Victorians were, however, vain and largely blind to the disease, cruelty and poverty which flourished and festered in the midst of contrasting affluence. Bent double in the mines, young lads became deformed through dragging heavy tubs of coal along the grim underground galleries. Climbing boys were still suffocating in crooked, soot-filled chimneys, while in the ghastly mills and factories youngsters were toiling for long hours in the most deplorable of circumstances. Throughout the Queen's reign efforts were certainly made to improve such conditions but, in the main, the Victorians could be criticised for not showing enough commitment to industrial and social reform. Quintin Hogg's personal crusade to further the cause of the deprived and persecuted did not, unfortunately, typify the attitude of his contemporaries.

While the fight to enhance the welfare of the poorer sections of the population was to prove a protracted and arduous struggle, football was mushrooming in popularity at a staggering rate. Although, in some cases, under the guise of now unfamiliar names, one by one the great clubs which would dominate the game in years to come were being spawned. The Arsenals, Evertons, Celtics and Manchester Uniteds of this world would, ironically, with the rapid growth of professionalism from the 1890s, provide a future escape route for many a young man who would otherwise have been condemned to a life of hard labour in the pits and in the steelworks.

But if we condemn those haughty Victorians for their insufferable pride, vanity and blindness, we must also acknowledge the fact that, in literary terms, they were their own most eloquent and outspoken critics. Thackeray in *Vanity Fair* and *The Book of Snobs* savaged his contemporaries, Dickens exposed their shocking neglect of social evils and Samuel Butler vehemently attacked the religious hypocrisy of the time. Where else but in Victorian Britain could a future Conservative Prime Minister, Disraeli, write a novel about the "Two nations, the rich and the poor"? Sounds familiar!

Organised football took root in this land of stark contrasts that was the United Kingdom during the reign of Queen Victoria and the vast majority of today's senior clubs sprang to life in that colourful age of great invention and innovation. Huge and powerful steam trains, which greedily devoured tons of that hard-earned coal, transported the footballers of the nineteenth century to and from matches on a vast network of railways. As they gazed out of the train windows across the smoke-filled landscape and dark Satanic mills of the Industrial Revolution, those moustachioed Victorian players could never have foreseen the changes which weren't really all that far around soccer's corner. Just a few months after the death of Quintin Hogg in 1903, American brothers, Wilbur and Orville Wright, successfully constructed and flew a petrol-driven biplane on the smooth, windswept sands of Kitty Hawk, North Carolina. Within a relatively short space of time the magic of flight would transport football players to hitherto inconceivable and far-flung hotbeds of soccer!

Described as a "dashing and resolute player", Quintin Hogg enjoyed football from his early schooldays until shortly before his death and, in the winter of 1902, when aged fifty-seven, played in a match for "The Old Quintonians" to enable him to establish a record of "fifty years of footer".

On the evening of 16 January 1903, as the Polytechnic Institute was closing for the night, Quintin stood at the top of the steps, shaking hands with members as they left. On noticing that one lad was very thinly clad, he asked, "Where's your overcoat this cold night, sonny?" The boy said that he didn't have one. Laying a hand on his shoulder, Hogg detained the lad while a porter went and got him a warm coat. Quintin helped the boy into the coat and buttoned it up before sending him home. Sadly, that was his last personal gesture towards his "boys". On entering his room the following morning, servants found Quintin Hogg lying dead in his bath. Initially it was thought he had died of heart failure, but death was subsequently proved to have been caused by asphyxiation from the fumes of a gas stove in the bathroom, for which adequate ventilation had not been provided.

Huge crowds attended his funeral to mourn the passing of a man whose wrinkled and gaunt features told the story of his anxious struggle and lifelong concern for the welfare of others. Older and very much wiser, the original lads from Quintin's "Ragged School" in "Of Alley" were present in significant numbers to pay their own last respects to a fine human being who had achieved miracles on their behalf and to whom they were so greatly indebted. Lying amidst the hundreds of wreaths was one from those boys, simply and movingly inscribed: "We loved him, but it was nothing to his wondrous love for us."

Arthur Kinnaird, who alone of all the governors of the game of football had lived through and greatly influenced every phase of the evolution of the sport over sixty years, died almost exactly twenty years later on 30 January 1923, aged seventy-five. Kinnaird's vision had played a significant part in the building of that great Empire Stadium at Wembley (or Imperial Stadium as it was then known). But although he lived long enough to see his dream realised, sadly the great man passed away just three months before a record crowd watched Bolton Wanderers beat West Ham United 2–0 in Wembley's first ever FA Cup Final, played on 28 April 1923.

An entire book would hardly be adequate to cover the remarkable life story of Kinnaird's closest friend, Quintin Hogg. Given that luxury, it would still prove impossible to do justice to the extent of the charitable work which this kind-hearted individual undertook. In this chapter I have, of necessity, only been able to scratch the surface of a great philanthropist's life, merely to give a brief insight into the mind of a Victorian gentleman who loved football along with his fellows and who left us all with a great legacy. A fitting conclusion is provided by the words of his friend, the Duke of Argyll, who was also involved with the ''Poly'' and who, on the death of Quintin Hogg in 1903, wrote:

> Such was our founder Quintin, generous, strong,
> Whether the fight was football or the mart,
> Where runs the current of the Empire's heart,
> He played the game, loved right and hated wrong.

4

THOSE LADS O' LEVEN'S VALE

Johnny Ferguson was a grand wee sportsman in the 1860s. He won almost all the prizes at the Sunday School sports in his home at Jamestown, Alexandria, which is situated in Dunbartonshire's Vale of Leven and virtually within the shadow of Ben Lomond. In his youth Johnny became a professional runner, or a pedestrian as professional runners were called before the advent of the twentieth century. Ferguson was a natural athlete and the young man lifted many a trophy at leading athletics events all over the country. His prowess on the track can be gauged by the fact that in January 1872 he won the prestigious mile event at Edinburgh's Powderhall Stadium in a then record time of four minutes sixteen and a half seconds.

In the late 1860s and early 1870s rugby and, to an even greater extent, shinty were the most popular sports in the Vale of Leven and, needless to say, Johnny and his pals were enthusiastic participants in those particular pastimes. Then fate took a hand and a new game came along . . . a new game which was to drastically change the lives of those sports-mad lads from the beautiful Leven Valley!

At that time Scotland's mother club, Queen's Park, was engaged in "missionary" work aimed at spreading association football in Scotland. In their travels, representatives of the famous "Spiders" "knocked on the door" of those shinty enthusiasts in Alexandria, asked them to abandon that game and to take up football. "Will you come and let us see it first?" was the immediate response. Queens were happy to agree and arranged a demonstration of the rapidly emerging sport. Suffice to say, the Vale lads were so impressed that in 1872 they decided to adopt the new fangled game, to form a club of their own and to call it Vale of Leven Football Club. Queen's Park couldn't have been trying too hard when they formally opened Vale's ground in March 1873 because the game ended 0–0 and was stopped several times so that the experts could explain the rules to the inexperienced Levenites.

However, those lads from that Dunbartonshire town did not lack experience for long. Johnny Ferguson and his chums had boundless energy for outdoor games and they embraced their new-found passion with tremendous enthusiasm. Sporting distinction usually takes some considerable time to attain and invariably proves to be an uphill struggle. But the meteoric rise of Vale of Leven Football Club, the peaks which they were so rapidly to climb and the comradeship which the players were to take with them to their graves, is one of football's greatest and most moving stories. Vale were, beyond doubt, Queen's Park's most brilliant pupils, and in no time at all the seed which the famous Crosshill club had sown was to grow and grow.

Despite the fact that Vale of Leven were, in 1873, one of the founder clubs of the Scottish Football Association and had donated £1 towards the cost of the Scottish Cup, they did not participate in the newly-formed competition for the first two years, scratching to Dumbarton and Clydesdale respectively. Apparently the Cup Committee insisted that professional runners, particularly our friend Johnny Ferguson, were prohibited from playing in the strictly amateur tournament and the Vale of Leven was a renowned "ped" stronghold. Happily the problem was resolved, because Vale did take part in the third competition and were beaten 2–1 by Queen's Park in the semi-final. But the following year they astounded everyone when that scoreline was reversed on the last Saturday of December 1876 in the fifth round of the Scottish Cup and Vale of Leven became the first Scottish side to beat Queen's Park since the famous Hampden club was founded over nine years earlier in 1867!

The Vale of Leven side which won the Scottish Cup for the first time in 1877. Back row left to right: W. Jamieson, A. Michie, W.C. Wood, A. McIntyre, A. McLintock. Front left to right: R. Paton, D. McGregor, D. Lindsay, J. Ferguson, J. McDougall, J. Baird.

Having leapt this seemingly impossible hurdle they went on to meet Rangers in the final and, after two drawn matches played at Hamilton Crescent, beat the Glasgow side 3–2 at First Hampden on Friday, 13 April 1877, to become the first provincial club to win, what was then, the undisputed "blue ribbon" of Scottish football . . . the Scottish Cup!

Glasgow's patron saint, St Mungo, couldn't have been too happy with the fact that Vale had beaten Third Lanark and Queen's Park earlier in the competition and, clearly, the poor fellow dropped his halo when shocked by the result of that particular Cup Final . . . as an anonymous and evidently delighted poet suggested in the *Dumbarton Herald* of 19 April 1877:

> "My plucky Rangers," Mungo cried,
> "Shall put The Vale to rout,
> And ere we leave the field tonight
> Their victory we'll shout . . .
> For all my sons do swear," quoth he,
> "Twill be a home team victory."
>
> With hoots and groans the crowd around
> The Vale men did deride,
> And many a curse from Mungo's mouth
> Was thrown . . . the ropes inside.
> But things like this . . . in town . . . must be,
> When Leven scores a victory.
>
> They say it was a saddening sight
> After the cup was won,
> For thousands then of Mungo's men,
> Were speechless every one,
> But things like this . . . in town . . . we see,
> When Leven gains the victory.

What a welcome awaited Johnny Ferguson, Bobby Paton, Andy McIntyre, Jackie Baird and the rest of those heroes when they arrived home in Alexandria with that wonderful trophy. The famous Bonhill Instrumental Band was playing at the railway station, the town centre fountain was in full spate and, as the victorious team were carried shoulder high down the station steps, the strains of *See the Conquering Hero Comes* could be heard as the musicians loudly sounded trumpets and beat drums in an effort to compete with the almost deafening roar of the crowd.

Vale retained the Scottish Cup the following year when they beat Third Lanark 1–0 in a Hampden final. Then, in 1879, Rangers were once again Vale's opponents and the club which stood between the Dunbartonshire boys and a hat-trick of Cup Final victories. The sides drew 1–1 and, although Rangers complained that the referee had disallowed "a perfectly good goal", the protest was over-ruled and a replay ordered. Rangers refused to play. So Vale turned up, solemnly lined up, kicked off and scored against a non-existent opposition before trooping off the field. That made it three Scottish Cup wins in a row and Vale of Leven had emulated their one-time masters, Queen's Park, who had won the trophy in the first three years of competition.

Despite their epic battles and their differences on the football field, Rangers and The Vale had developed a healthy respect and admiration for each other. In particular Johnny Ferguson, by now a dashing and exciting Vale forward, and Rangers' full-back and captain, Tom Vallance, had struck up what was to prove an enduring friendship. Like Ferguson, Tom Vallance was a native of The Vale and a top-class athlete, as he demonstrated in 1881 at the Queen's Park sports when setting a Scottish long jump record (21 feet 11 inches) which stood for fourteen years. One of the founders of Glasgow Rangers, Tom was also a gifted artist and had two of his paintings accepted by the Royal Scottish Academy. Both men represented Scotland on several occasions, Johnny being the first provincial player to be selected for his country when he played in the Scottish team which, in beating England 2–1 at Hamilton Crescent in 1874, recorded Scotland's first victory over that "Auld Enemy". Later, in 1877, Johnny and Tom were team-mates in the Scottish international sides which won two matches within the space of three days. England were beaten 3–1 at the Oval on 3 March, with Ferguson scoring twice and, two days later, Wales were defeated 2–0 at Wrexham.

In recognition of Vale's first cup success, a local firm had donated a beautiful silver trophy called The Loving Cup to the heroes of the successful Vale of Leven side, the condition being that it would be held by each of the players for one year at a time and that the last survivor should keep the cup and pass it on to his family or, alternatively, bequeath it to some institution in The Vale. "Bauldie" of *The Scottish Referee*, writing on the subject in June 1905, had this to say:

> I do not, nor does anyone, happily, know who is to be the last survivor on old Earth's solid ba, but whoever he be, I am sure that his latter days will be cheered and solaced by the many happy memories which are associated with this cup of cups, and on which is inscribed . . . shall I say for all time? . . . the names of the lads in red and blue who made Leven's Vale so famous in Scottish football history.

While Vale of Leven were achieving so much success north of the border their English counterparts, the famous Wanderers from London, were sweeping all before them. Having won the FA Cup five times in the 1870s, Wanderers challenged the Scottish club to travel to the Capital and to play them at Kennington Oval. The English side had already beaten Queen's Park and their reputation was awe-inspiring, so those "guid folk o' the Vale" were more than a little apprehensive as to the possible outcome of such an encounter. But, possessing the minds to dare and the will to do, the Dunbartonshire boys accepted the challenge and on the evening of 11 April 1878 set off on their great adventure. *Dumbarton Herald* reporter, John Miller, who travelled with the party, takes up the story:

The team accompanied by a few friends, left Alexandria on Thursday evening at 7 p.m. in a special carriage, per N.B. Railway, via East Coast route for London. A considerable crowd assembled at the station, and loudly cheered the departure of the train. A number of friends also witnessed the departure of the team from Glasgow at 8.50 p.m., and wished them a hearty "good-bye". Before Edinburgh was reached the team had established a system of communication between the separate compartments of the carriage by the windows, the result of which was that messages and refreshments of all kinds were freely passed to and from each member of the party. Indeed we doubt if the Vale ever played a better "passing game". The right wing passed well to the centre, who, in turn, passed to the left wing, in the most unselfish manner. At Edinburgh a brief promenade was enjoyed on the platform, during which the team and their friends were the observed of all observers. One gentleman of the party, a proficient performer on a penny whistle, kindly favoured them with a selection of popular airs on that wonderful instrument. Another looked quite picturesque in a bright striped night cap, while a third, with an enormous worsted Tam O' Shanter and a tiger skin rug, placidly smoked a pipe curiously carved from the branch of a tree, to the amazement of the sober-sided "Capitalists". Berwick was reached at midnight, and here the party danced a reel in costume to the wonder of the sleepy officials.

It's more like the description of a twentieth-century supporters' club outing to Wembley before they banned the booze, than that of the Scottish Cup holders travelling to play the FA Cup winners and the pride of English football in their own back yard, isn't it? John Miller paints a wonderfully vivid and, indeed, poetic picture of the next stage of that historic trip to London:

Off again, and in a few minutes the Tweed was crossed, the moon shining brightly on its rippling waters, as they flow into the German Ocean, which comes rolling in white breakers to the shore. An endeavour was afterwards made to snatch forty-winks, but the wakeful would not permit the drowsy god to close the eyes of those who could and so the "wee short hour ayont the twal" crept on as the express dashed through the landscape, all bathed in moonlight, until we halted at Newcastle at 1.50 a.m., and were unexpectedly welcomed at this unearthly hour by the sight of a party of enthusiastic natives of the Vale rushing to shake hands with the team and wish them success. What a five minutes followed, and what a ringing cheer was sent after the departing train can better be imagined than described.

When the happy band finally arrived at King's Cross station on the Friday morning they were somewhat travel-weary and, no doubt, some of them were nursing a hangover. However, after booking into their hotel, a good wash and a big breakfast, they were off sightseeing in London and visiting Madame Tussaud's, the Tower of London and the zoo. Believe it or not, the boys actually went to bed early that evening and the following morning, after watching Oxford easily beat Cambridge in the thirty-fifth University Boat Race, Johnny Ferguson and his mates headed for Kennington Oval and their much-publicised confrontation with the Wanderers. Those "country" lads really lived for football and clearly enjoyed the game as it should be enjoyed.

Although their build-up to the match could in no sense be described as "professional", the outcome of what was, come to think of it, a Cup Winners' Cup final, gave Scottish football one of its greatest ever victories. Despite the fact that the game was played under the English throw-in rule, Vale triumphed by three goals to one, with Johnny Ferguson playing his finest game for the club and scoring a hat-trick. The Wanderers entertained the victorious Scots to dinner that evening and the toast was pledged in the FA Cup by the Wanderers captain and Scottish internationalist, none other than our old friend . . . The Honourable Arthur Fitzgerald Kinnaird!

Sadly, after their great achievements in the 1870s, Vale of Leven Football Club plunged into comparatively rapid decline and, although they figured in four more Scottish Cup finals, they were never to reach such dizzy heights again. However, the beautiful Loving Cup helped to ensure that those lads of the Old Vale teams retained a deeply-rooted bond of affection for each other, which was to last for the rest of their days.

Way back in the 1870s a little lad called James Ferguson (no relation) had watched enthralled as his heroes in red and blue marched from triumph to triumph. Those marvellous Vale of Leven players had greatly enriched his life and that little lad never forgot them. James became a very successful and wealthy London businessman and, in the 1920s, organised and financed annual reunions of the surviving members of the Old Vale teams. Many a happy day was enjoyed on trips to such places as Turnberry Hotel and Loch Lomond, as the heroes and countless friends from the world of football enjoyed this kindly man's hospitality. The Loving Cup exchanged hands on those trips and a souvenir brochure was presented to the guests on each outing.

From the Bronze by the late F. Derwent Wood, R. A.

The Old Vale reunion at Loch Lomond on 1 September 1928 was particularly pleasurable as, with the sun shining brightly, well over one hundred guests enjoyed a sail on the steamer *Prince Edward* and were wined and dined in a manner befitting the occasion. John McDowall, Secretary of the Scottish Football Association for a remarkable forty-six years, prepared a speech for the occasion of that Old Vale outing to Loch Lomond. Sadly he was too ill to attend and died just five days after the event, on 6 September 1928. But this great Burns lover's reference to James Ferguson's generosity and the parallel which he drew in that never delivered, written speech makes interesting reading:

It is said that Betty Davidson, who resided with the Burns family when the poet was a child, used to tell wonderful ghost stories and fairy tales, when sitting around the ingle, which Robert eagerly listened to and greedily drank in. This old woman deserves the gratitude of posterity for unconsciously fanning into flame the newly kindled spark of genius in the boy's developing intelligence and, had it not been for her, we would not have had the matchless effusions of *Hallowe'en*, the *Address to the Deil'*, or the immortal *Tam o' Shanter*.

Johnny McDowall . . .
a great Burns lover!

Rabbie Burns . . . photograph
reproduced by kind permission of
the Scottish Tourist Board.

In like manner, there was a football team on the banks of the Leven, who, by their prowess, charmed the natives, kindled the enthusiasm of the countryside and brought honour and glory to the town in which resided a wee boy who drank it all in and instinctively begot an enthusiasm and love for the heroes, and, when fortune favoured him, this man, of their own kith and kin, in the goodness of his heart and the richness of his soul, and in the deep sympathy of his nature, has brought us together year after year to commemorate these immortal days.

It is said . . . when the power of imparting joy is equal to the will, the human soul requires no other heaven.

Sir Walter Scott said . . . "One crowded hour of glorious life is worth an age without a name."

How many hours of glorious life has our host given us!

Football is deeply indebted to Mr Ferguson. We are all in a lasting indebtedness to him.

We all know Mr Ferguson as a sportsman and a man of high ideals. He has grasped the essence of sportsmanship. He knows:

> When the last great scorer
> Comes to write against his name,
> He'll write not that he won or lost,
> But how he played the game.

Those gatherings which James Ferguson arranged were splendid occasions with many a wee dram being enjoyed in memory of those glorious days in the 1870s and, doubtless, there was more than one toast to the lads from Queen's Park who had first persuaded Johnny Ferguson and his pals to give up shinty and to take up football. Tom Vallance, who had become a successful restaurateur in Glasgow as well as President of Rangers from 1883–1889, was an honoured guest at most of those Old Vale reunions. Tom, himself a Burns enthusiast, wrote this touching adaptation of Rabbie's song *John Anderson, My Jo, John* in 1926 and gave it to his long time pal, Johnny Ferguson, "In remembrance of fifty years of friendship on and off the football field":

Johnny Ferguson in his playing days.

John Ferguson, my frien' John,
When we were first aquaint,
Your comely heid had hair on't,
But noo its unco scant;
Your sturdy legs were soople then . . .
You could run like any fawn,
But, whatever ails your auld shanks noo?
John Ferguson, my John!

Tom Vallance.

John Ferguson, my frien' John,
We've played fitba' thegither,
And often did we try, John,
To dodge and jink each ither.
But tho' noo oor jinkin's done, John,
Oor tongues can still wag on,
It would try you sair, if yours wagged nae mair,
John Ferguson, my John!

John Ferguson, my frien' John,
What pleasure did it gie
To a' your frien's around the ring
While makin' rings round me.
But it didna aye come aff, John,
For my legs were whiles too long,
And I'll play you yet, if new legs ye get,
John Ferguson, my John!

John Ferguson, my frien' John,
When you to heaven will gang,
Or will it be the ither place?
But sure you'll no gang wrang.
But, whichever place it be, John,
You will tell them the auld, auld tale,
That you are the best fitba' player
That ever cam' frae the Vale.

Johnny Ferguson in the late 1920s.

Tom Vallance when an old man.

John Ferguson, my frien' John,
When you first played the game,
You had a staunch and hardy team
Wha brocht the Vale to fame . . .
But they're maistly gone before you John,
And we hope they'll have lang to wait
For the day of the great reception
They're gieing ye at the Golden Gate.

John Ferguson, my frien' John,
We've climbed life's hill thegither,
And many a happy day like this,
We've spent wi' yin an' ither . . .
But, tho' we're tottering doon noo, John
For the "Loving Cup" haud on,
Tho' the race is long you're still going strong,
John Ferguson, my John!

In describing Johnny Ferguson as the greatest player who ever came from the Vale of Leven, Tom Vallance was paying his pal a huge tribute because Dumbarton and Renton also hailed from the Vale, were counted among Scotland's strongest sides before the turn of the century and, in common with Vale of Leven Football Club, had supplied many great players to Scotland's international side.

At that Old Vale outing to Loch Lomond in September 1928, Tom Vallance, in proposing the toast to the Old Vale team, said that he had read in a spiritualist paper that football was played in Heaven and that he earnestly hoped that this was the case, as Heaven without football would hold little attraction for him. He remembered that, in the old days after a match, the Vale and the Rangers players used to meet in Jamie Kinloch's public house and that, therein, they enjoyed the finest pies that money could buy. If there was a celestial Jamie Kinloch's public house in the next world, Tom hoped that his friend, Johnny Ferguson, would bring the Loving Cup with him.

Those bonnie, bonnie banks o' Loch Lomond.

Sadly, the one-time rivals and long-time pals never met again on those bonnie, bonnie banks of Loch Lomond. But it's nice to surmise that the Old Vale and the Old Rangers and especially Johnny and Tom are, even now, reliving their fund of football memories. Perhaps they and their team-mates are, at last, deciding the issue of that unplayed Scottish Cup final replay of

Alexander Jamieson's painting of the Titus Arch in Rome.

1879. Or maybe they are, at this moment, enjoying a pie and a pint in Jamie's heavenly public house.

As was the custom, each guest at that outing in 1928 was presented with a souvenir brochure as a memento of an unforgettable day. Included within its pages was a colour reproduction of a painting by Alexander Jamieson, which was the pride of James Ferguson's private collection. The survivors of the Old Vale team would readily testify to the fact that the words on the canvas were indicative of James's own philosophy of life. Here is the description of the painting as printed in that souvenir:

> The treatment of the design is that of the Titus Arch in Rome, commonly known as the Triumphal Arch of the Caesars. Sunken with age, while old Rome has fallen beside it, it is surmounted by a group in bronze of Triumph in his chariot surrounded by his attendant Angels looking out over the Tiber as it goes to the sea. In the distant landscape are the hills and the road of the Appian Way. The arch is marble, stained and discoloured with age. The spandrels are figures in relief representing Virtue and Fame, supporting the keystone. Coming from under the arch and climbing over the rough road on a powerful horse is a man of middle age and swarthy complexion, well armed for the battle of life and strong in health and power; hat in hand, he expresses the noble sentiment:
> "I shall pass through this world but once. Any good thing that I can do or any kindness that I can show any human being, let me do it now and not defer it . . . for I shall not pass this way again."

Unfortunately, in today's predominantly greedy, selfish and "win at all costs" society, men like James Ferguson are the exception rather than the rule. Why can't we all show a little more kindness and, as far as football is concerned, follow Ferguson's example and keep a watchful eye on the welfare of the great masters of yesteryear? Without their tremendous contribution to our national sport, just where would football be today? Palatial stadiums with lavishly furnished boardrooms are, when all is said and done, no more than "but and bens", because football is really about the skills and emotions of human beings. We could learn a great deal from those Old Vale players and from the attitudes of men like James Ferguson and Tom Vallance to life in general and to our beloved sport in particular. I am certain that, were they around today, they would shake their heads in sadness and disbelief on observing some of the despicable attitudes which pollute the modern game. The message from the dim and distant past is crystal clear . . . so let's set the ball rolling and follow their example and philosophy. Let's endeavour to put the smile back on football's face and not delay it, for only one thing is certain . . . when our final whistle is blown, there is no possibility of a replay or extra-time in this individual game called life.

The Old Vale players have all passed through this world and slipped away quietly into the pages of football history. Sadly, those mortals who gained immortality through their exploits on the football field are now long gone. But their "cup of cups" will endure for all time and will, as much as anything else, ensure that the names of those heroes will live forever.

In 1900 Johnny Ferguson abandoned his vocation as a stane dyke builder and moved to Kilmarnock to become a publican. He settled in that Ayrshire town and was a frequent visitor to Kilmarnock FC's Rugby Park ground, where he became an enthusiastic fan and season-ticket holder. He attended the Scotland versus England match played at Ibrox on 5 April 1902 and narrowly avoided being killed when a section of the west terracing collapsed hurling twenty-five fans to their deaths. Ferguson was indeed fortunate not to be counted among the dead or almost 600 injured, on an occasion when the 1–1 scoreline and the fact that, for the first time in the series, no amateur player was included in either line-up was almost wholly ignored in the deluge of after-match newspaper coverage which chronicled the disaster.

By the late 1920s the one-time champion of the Sunday School sports was old, bent, more than a little deaf and suffering from arthritis. But, as ever, Johnny loved his football and, distinctive with ear trumpet and walking-stick, was a popular and familiar figure at Rugby Park, where he delighted many a fan by recounting tales of his playing days.

James Ferguson was a frequent visitor to Johnny's Bridge Inn bar and Glebe Road home. To the amazement of wide-eyed locals, James would draw up in a huge chauffeur-driven Rolls-Royce and whisk his long-time hero off on an impromptu drive down the coast followed by a slap-up lunch in a five-star hotel. Or, if operating on a tight business schedule while in Scotland, he would simply call in to pay his respects and drop off a box of the best cigars.

In 1929 Kilmarnock won the Scottish Cup for the second time in the decade and a delighted Johnny Ferguson was a welcome guest at the club's celebrations. I'll bet there was a tear in the old man's eye when, once again, he held the trophy which had changed his life and which had meant so much to the great friends and team-mates who had gone before him. Yes . . . the lad from the Leven Valley and that wonderful Scottish Cup were reunited and, ironically, it was Rangers that "Killie" had beaten 2–0 in the Hampden final.

Johnny didn't live long enough to be the last custodian of that other fabulous trophy, the Loving Cup. He passed away on 6 September 1929, in his eighty-first year, a few months after Kilmarnock's famous victory, and after a last-minute goal by Aberdeen's Alex Cheyne in Scotland's 1–0 victory over England had signalled the birth of that "Roar" at the third Hampden he had known.

Full-back Andy McIntyre, who died in 1941 and played in all three of Vale's cup successes, was the last survivor on "old Earth's solid ba". McIntyre's relatives must have presented the Loving Cup to the people of the Vale of Leven, but the cup was "lost" for many years and only comparatively recently did its silver again catch the light of day. While endeavouring to find the trophy I was fortunate enough to talk to Gerard Cairns, then Head Librarian at Alexandria library. Gerard was enthralled with my story and, with admirable enthusiasm, traced the "anonymous" and dust-covered cup to a cupboard in the library headquarters at Dumbarton.

That Loving Cup now belongs to the people of Scotland. It's a cup of friendship, a cup of remembrance, a cup whose shining silver mirrors the success of a great football club. But it is also a cup of patriotism for its truly remarkable story accurately reflects the characteristics of the Scottish people.

Unfortunately the name of Vale of Leven no longer figures in the forefront of Scottish football. In the wake of a number of disastrous seasons, they vanished from the scene in season 1892–93, returned in 1905 and remained in the league until the outbreak of the Great War in 1914. Vale made yet another come back in 1921 and, sadly, played their last senior game in 1928. But, happily, Vale of Leven Juniors still proudly keep the name and traditions of the old club alive. In 1953, amid great excitement, they recreated the glory days when they defeated Annbank United 1–0 in the Scottish Junior Cup final at Hampden.

If, as reputed, the ghost of Arsenal's famous manager, Herbert Chapman, nightly stalks the marbled halls of Highbury, and if the spirit of Johnny Thomson stands proudly in Glasgow Celtic's goal, then surely an imperishable halo of glory surrounds the memory of those lads in red and blue who did so much for the advancement of the game of football and who, all those years ago, first took the Scottish Cup out of Glasgow and home to that beautiful valley where the winding Leven flows.

5

WATTIE OF THE AUBURN LOCKS

Among those souvenirs in that wonderful attic of mine can be found a very special pair of antique football boots and some international badges which belonged to a man who was one of the sport's all-time greats . . . a man who had the name *Walter Arnott* etched on his birth certificate.

The son of a Glasgow corn merchant, Walter was born on 12 May 1861 and lived with his parents, three sisters and brother in St Andrew's Drive, part of the city's Pollokshields district. From a very early age the little auburn-haired boy demonstrated an aptitude for ball games . . . an aptitude which was to blossom and see the lad grow up to become the flower of Scotland's sporting heroes. Rugby was Wattie's first love but, happily, that sport never flourished on the South Side of Glasgow and, despite the fact that he was compelled to play rugby at Glasgow High School, it wasn't long before the youngster shunned the rugger field for the more refined skills of football.

In November 1872, when just eleven years old, Walter heard that Scotland and England were to meet for the first time in a big international and the little lad was filled with a burning desire to be present at the occasion. But how could little Walter and his pals get to the Hamilton Crescent venue, which was sited in a place called Partick, five miles away on the other side of the bustling river Clyde? Nothing, but nothing, was going to prevent Walter Arnott from getting to that historic game. So, on the morning of the big day and accompanied by a few friends, the little chap ventured forth to tramp the road and the miles to the match venue, the West of Scotland cricket ground in Hamilton Crescent.

But disappointment lay in store for those young explorers because, on reaching their destination, the lads were shocked to discover that they were expected to pay the huge sum of one shilling to gain admittance to the ground. What few coppers the boys had brought with them had been squandered somewhere along the way, and so it was a desperate little group who begged a cab driver to help them see the game by allowing them to climb on to the roof of his horse-drawn cab. Happily the "cabby" agreed and it was from that unusual perch that little Walter witnessed Scotland's first attempt to defeat her "New Enemy", England, on that St Andrew's Day Saturday way back in 1872. The Scottish side was composed entirely of Queen's Park players and the excitement which the occasion generated, fuelled by the skills of men like Jamie Weir, who was known as "The Prince of Dribblers", captivated Walter Arnott and left a deeply-rooted impression.

It's a lovely little picture, isn't it? The eleven-year-old lad standing on top of that horse-drawn cab, transfixed by the talents of those early international players who fought out a 0–0 draw on a never-to-be-forgotten occasion. Wattie didn't know then that, in days to come, he would play in a record ten consecutive matches against those awesome, yet impressive, Englishmen. He could never have imagined that he was to win three Scottish Cup winner's medals with Queen's Park and play for the Hampden club in two FA Cup Finals. That wide-eyed kid would never have believed that, one fine day, the name and fame of Walter Arnott would become as well known, esteemed and respected, as much in the rest of the United Kingdom, as within the borders of his native land.

When Walter left school he joined the now long-defunct Pollokshields Athletic and, while a member of that club, was selected by the Scottish FA to play for Glasgow against Sheffield. But the following year Arnott moved to Queen's Park and this was to prove a significant development in his career. In 1883 he was selected as reserve for the England match and in the same year the full-back played for Scotland for the first time when the Scots beat Wales 3–0 at Wrexham. For reasons best known to himself, Arnott returned to Pollokshields Athletic, taking over the captaincy of the club, and for some time his loyalties were divided between his first love and Queen's Park. Clearly neither club relished such a situation and Arnott was forced to decide where his football future lay. Walter opted for Queen's, a fact which is indelibly recorded in the history of Scottish football.

On 26 January 1884, he captained the Scottish side which beat Ireland 5–0 in the first international match between the nations. Although Walter Arnott was greatly honoured to represent his country against those lads from the "Emerald Isle" and the boys from "The Valleys", there was only one international contest which really mattered in those days and that was the annual fixture against . . . you know who! On 15 March 1884, a date which Walter Arnott was never to forget, the wee boy's dream became a reality when the lettering on the badge of his Scottish jersey read "England 1884". Clearly relishing the opportunity to recall the occasion within the pages of a Scottish newspaper in April 1931, and just a month before he died, Walter wrote:

> The first time that I had the honour of playing for my beloved Scotland in the "big international" was on old Cathkin Park, in Govanhill, in season 1883–84. In the days of my boyhood, in watching international matches, I simply revered the names of the "giants of football" who took part in these games. I had witnessed Jamie Weir completely bewilder the enemy by sheer cleverness; and seen MacDougall, MacGregor, Johnny Ferguson, and other Vale of Leven

The great Walter Arnott.

stalwarts astound everybody by their successful dash and daring; watched and admired Charlie Campbell of Queen's Park leap in the air and head the ball away from the goalmouth when everything seemed lost; and shouted myself hoarse with ecstatic joy when that wonderful Queen's Park centre forward, ·George Ker, scored goals that no opposition could save. One can therefore imagine with what feelings of determination I stepped on to Cathkin Park that afternoon in 1884 to fight my country's battle.

And what a battle lay ahead of the Queen's Park defender, because he was directly opposed to that famous English forward, Charlie Bambridge of the Swifts as well as the towering six foot four inch figure of William Gunn, the renowned Nottinghamshire cricketer and Notts County footballer. William Pickford, a famous referee who later became President of the Football

Association as well as a respected football writer, was at the match and, over twenty years on, recalled Walter Arnott's stirring performance:

> Arnott's partner on that occasion was John Forbes, the old Vale of Leven player, and though the latter was justly reckoned one of the finest full-backs ever seen, he had that day to be content with second place to Wattie of the auburn locks. Arnott was then in his prime and so was William Gunn of Notts County. The duel between those two giants of the game was a thing to be forever remembered. I have never seen a forward play finer football than William Gunn did on that day. Ably assisted by E.C. Bambridge, another famous forward, Gunn frequently swept the field from end to end with the ball at his toe. He dodged and feinted and ran as no man ever ran before or since. He was without doubt incomparably the greatest forward on the field that day. I have said that

Gunn frequently swept the field from end to end, but that statement requires qualification. Gunn was irresistible until he came within the Scottish twenty-five, when he and Arnott between them played the most dramatic duel ever witnessed. With his long raking strides Gunn came tearing up the touchline, evading with something like ease the Scottish forwards and half-backs. All went well until he came within the sphere of Arnott's influence, which on this occasion might be likened to the torrid zone. On that day great as Gunn was, he met his master in Walter Arnott. Gunn himself would be the first to acknowledge it, and he would do so without shame. To be beaten by Arnott in his prime was something to be proud of rather than resented. I give it as a fact that not more than twice during the ninety minutes of the game did Gunn even temporarily give Arnott the slip. He had either to part with the ball, or attempt to shoot over his head, and long shots were simple playthings to the great McAulay, who kept goal for Scotland.

That English side of 1884 laid the foundations of a football pattern which was to endure for decades, playing two full-backs, three half-backs and five forwards, while the Scots stuck to the then familiar format of two full-backs, two half-backs and six forwards.

It was an impressive English XI which represented their country at Cathkin. From all accounts they were a grand-looking side who, according to a newspaper report of the time, "made the Scots look like schoolboys". But those "schoolboys" were made of stern stuff and the result was "just what the doctor ordered" from a Scottish viewpoint, because, following "a long drive to the English goal by Arnott", Dr John Smith of Queen's Park scored the game's only goal when the match was just seven minutes old . . . and the Scots had recorded five successive victories over those most deadly of foes!

Walter Arnott was, by now, firmly entrenched in the Scottish defence and throughout the following nine years his face was never missing from a Scottish line-up versus England. In all, the Queen's Park man played fourteen times for his country and made eleven appearances for Glasgow in inter-city matches. As already mentioned, he won three Scottish Cup winner's medals with the "Spiders" and played in the Queen's sides which were beaten by Blackburn Rovers at Kennington Oval in both the 1883–84 and 1884–85 FA Cup Finals.

Nobody can possibly describe Walter Arnott's attributes more eloquently than his contemporary, William Pickford:

Walter Arnott was a giant amongst giants. Not only was he the best defender, but he was also the most artistic back I have ever seen and no one ever equalled the ease and elegance of his methods. Arnott as I remember him, was about medium height, thick set, with a magnificent back and chest, and legs that were made to kick. For a man of his stocky build, his pace was remarkable. He seemed to have no difficulty keeping pace with the fastest forward, and when he made a sudden rush at an opponent, he moved like a whirlwind. He was, I believe, one of the first backs to make a habit of placing the ball accurately to his forwards. I have seen him kick with such precision with his back turned towards his objective, that he seemed to have eyes in the back of his head. With fair hair curling down on his forehead, a bonnie blue eye that bore no man malice, and a face the embodiment of good-nature, Arnott was always a pleasing and picturesque figure. There were many noted forwards who could make no headway at all against the famous Queen's Park player. I remember Sandilands, the Old Westminster and Corinthian player, once telling me that he simply could do nothing against Arnott. This was a few days after the game between the Corinthians and Queen's Park at Leyton, when the famous Pink forward, then in his prime, found Arnott a terrible stumbling block. He more than hinted that Arnott had a mesmeric influence over him. It certainly seemed so. Every time that Sandilands approached the great Scottish back he stood still, apparently petrified, and the ball seemed to pass by some occult influence from the Londoner to the sturdy Scot. Many another famous forward had paid Arnott a similar compliment.

I wonder if Walter Arnott's hypnotic influence on opposing forwards would have been as effective if confronted with the mesmerising skills of Stanley Matthews or the brilliant trickery and electrifying pace of the "Preston Plumber", Tom Finney? How would he have fared if confronted with the jinking genius of Jimmy Johnstone or the magic which has been weaved by that modern-day football conjurer, Davie Cooper of Rangers? And, given the chance, could Walter have delved into his box of tricks and cast a spell on the one who, for me, was the greatest of them all . . . that lithe and tantalising football leprechaun from Ireland, Georgie Best? We will never know, will we? But one thing is for sure; Arnott would have dearly relished the challenge and I'm certain in my own mind that, were he still around today, there would be a place within the heart of the Scottish defence for "Wattie of the auburn locks".

His playing days over, Arnott became a representative for a confectionery firm and also developed into a fine football writer and after-dinner speaker. As the years passed, more and more of his time was spent at Millport on the Isle of Cumbrae where, amidst the beautiful Clyde coast scenery, he was able to pursue a long-standing passion for yachting.

Walter passed away in May 1931, just a few days after his seventieth birthday. When the remains of Walter Arnott were buried at Cathcart Cemetery in Glasgow on 21 May, a large crowd mourned the passing of the doyen of

Stanley Matthews
. . . mesmerising skills!

Peerless Tom Finney
. . . "The Preston Plumber".

George Best . . . arguably the
greatest footballer of all time!

Jimmy Johnstone . . . a jinking genius!

Scottish football and stood at a graveside covered by wreaths bearing the emblems of almost every football club in the land. Incidentally, it is sad to note that, when members of the Arnott family returned to the scene on the evening of the funeral, they were horrified to discover that the grave had been vandalised by souvenir hunters who had ripped those club badges from the garlands of flowers.

If only those famous old leather boots could talk! What a tale they would tell of that stupendous player with the "bonnie blue eye", who wore them with such style and distinction all those years ago. Wattie's favourite football boots served him well in many a historic match and perhaps they are worthy of a more dignified resting place. But this "attic fanatic" will always treasure them and, when the time comes for him to greet the great Walter Arnott in the next world, he'll make very sure that the badges, photographs and historic football boots which belonged to a sporting "giant amongst giants" will survive to bring pleasure to future generations and to ensure that the story of that adventurous little lad from Pollokshields will live forever. In the meantime that famous football footwear will be well cared for and kept highly polished. However, those little bits of earth and dried grass which cling tenaciously to the worn studs will never be removed . . . because there are fragments of old Cathkin and traces of Kennington Oval competing for loft space in a football shrine!

Walter Arnott and those treasured boots and badges.

6

THE ALL-BLACKS AT HAMPDEN

Hampden Park, the true home of football, celebrated its eighty-fifth birthday in 1988 . . . and what glories this ever-changing octogenarian has witnessed throughout those eight and a half decades! Scotland's national stadium has played host to the greatest international and club sides in the history of world soccer. The magical Magyars from Hungary, those colourful, multi-talented Brazilians and the finest club side ever, the incomparable and unforgettable, Real Madrid . . . to mention just a few. Names such as those conjure up images and rekindle memories of football played at the very highest level.

Likewise, devotees of that other game played with a strangely shaped ball, recall with pleasure and admiration the exploits of, for instance, the Red Dragons from Wales, those flamboyant Frenchmen and the most revered name in that sport and winners of rugby's first ever World Cup in June 1987 . . . the All-Blacks.

But apart from the fact that the Brazilians and the New Zealanders enjoy international acclaim for having set the very highest standards in their respective sports, they also share the distinction of having been honoured guests at the home of Queen's Park Football Club, Hampden Park! Yes, on Wednesday, 22 November 1905, to be precise, the All-Blacks played a Glasgow and West of Scotland select at the third and greatest Hampden, which was then only two years old.

On the previous Saturday, at Inverleith in Edinburgh, Scotland's international side had played marvellously well against New Zealand when losing by a slender 12–7 margin. Apart from enjoying a fiercely contested and very entertaining rugby match, the 21,000 crowd in the Scottish capital had been intrigued by the famous pre-match Maori war dance, the Haka, which was originally devised to instil fear into the hearts of enemies but, on rugby fields throughout the United Kingdom and elsewhere, has come to be regarded as a popular gesture of sportsmanlike defiance by a team far from home. That Inverleith crowd was also treated to the Maori war chant which starts *Ka*

Mate, Ka Mate, Ka Ora, Ka Ora, and was an ancient ditty which Maoris back from war sang as they danced around the bodies of their unfortunate victims before a cannibalistic feast.

Cannibals the 1905 All-Blacks were certainly not, but rugby players of the very highest calibre they most certainly were. Interestingly, a New Zealander, Nolan Fell, who had already played for Scotland on seven occasions while

The first All-Blacks.

studying medicine at Edinburgh University, was selected to play for Scotland against his old country. Fell refused to turn out against his fellow countrymen and Louis Greig, who was not named until the morning of the match, took his place. Greig later became equerry to the Duke of York (the future King George VI) whom he partnered in the doubles at Wimbledon in 1926 . . . but back to those colourful All-Blacks and their visit to the home of football!

Hampden Park was the venue for the twenty-first match of their British tour and, with twenty outright wins behind them, nobody gave the Scots the slightest chance of victory while, naturally, the tourists were extremely confident that they could extend their unbeaten run. On the Monday following the Scotland match the New Zealanders arrived in Glasgow where, on their first evening in the city, they visited the Hippodrome Theatre as guests of the owner and saw the ''world renowned'' actress, Minnie Palmer, appear in a

Hampden Park as it was in 1905.

revue called *Orange Nell*. Next day the lads went sight-seeing and later, on the eve of the match, they were back at the theatre . . . the Empire this time and a play entitled *The Road to Ruin*; a title which was certainly to prove ominous for their Hampden opponents.

On the following afternoon a 10,000 crowd, boosted by children who had been given the half-day from Glasgow's so-called "leading schools" to attend the match, watched the teams kick off in a biting wind and driving rain. It was widely acknowledged that the event would have attracted a huge crowd had it been played on a Saturday. However, the spectators were well entertained and the game, as expected, was of a "one-sided character", with the men in black not only dwarfing the Glasgow pack, but proving far too strong for them in a 22-0 win. From all accounts the tourists were speedy and clever and the Scots were apparently unable to cope with their all-round brilliance. According to a report in the following morning's *Glasgow Herald*: "Superb tackling, a remarkable combination of skill and strength, an amazing ability to pass at full speed and unceasing movement in the maul", were the most notable features of their play; features which brought them two goals and four tries and, in those days, accounted for their twenty-two-point total, a margin described in a *Herald* headline as "A Big Victory for the Colonials".

Throughout the UK interest aroused by the first ever official All-Blacks tour of Great Britain was overwhelming and, to coincide with their visit, newspapers and magazines carried adverts expounding the benefits of life in New Zealand, which was described as "the land of settlers". Assisted passage "down under" could be obtained for as little as £15 "to persons possessing small capital and approved by the High Commissioner". How many Scots emigrated, lured by the mouth-watering prospect of watching New Zealand rugby on a regular basis or, perhaps, sickened by the fact that Scotland's footballers had been beaten 1-0 by England in the two previous internationals between the countries, will never be known!

The *Glasgow Herald* of the time also carried reports of severe unemployment in Japan, stories of riots in the Russian city of St Petersburg (now Leningrad) and, on the advertising pages, offers of twelve worsted football jerseys for a mere 28s/6d post free, or a pair of top quality winter boots for the princely sum of 9s/11d. Changed days! Incidentally, Aston Villa were FA Cup holders, having won the competition for the fourth time by virtue of a 2–0 victory over Newcastle United in the 1905 final and Third Lanark won the Scottish Cup by beating Rangers 3–1 at Hampden in a Cup final replay.

During that historic United Kingdom tour of 1905–06, the All-Blacks played thirty-two matches, winning on thirty-one occasions and losing only once when, in front of an ecstatic 40,000 crowd, Wales beat the tourists 3–0 in Cardiff. During their trail of triumph around the British Isles the New Zealanders ran up a staggering total of 830 points against only thirty-nine and their line was crossed only seven times, whereas they themselves scored 215 tries (including one game in France) at an average of over six per match. Given those statistics and considering that both England and Ireland were comprehensively beaten by the same 15–0 scoreline, the narrow margin of Scotland's defeat represented a very commendable performance indeed. Nor had that select side which lost at Hampden any reason to feel too downhearted, for those classy "Colonials" had completely demolished most of Britain's top sides. For example, Oxford University and Hartlepool must have felt that they had been hit by a cyclone when they were trounced 47–0 and 63–0 respectively.

It is inconceivable that Hampden Park will ever again play host to the New Zealand rugby team. But it should never be forgotten that, on a wet Wednesday afternoon in 1905, those first official All-Black tourists earned the undeniable right to be counted among the footballers of Brazil, Hungary and elsewhere . . . as one of the greatest international sides which ever trod the hallowed turf of Hampden Park!

7

FOOD FOR THOUGHT

Now that hot take-away food is subject to Value Added Tax, it's costing us that bit more at the "chippie" for a traditional fish or pudding supper and we're having to dig a bit more deeply into our pockets to pay for that egg foo yung or beef chop suey carry-out from our local Chinese take-away. Food, glorious food. Not only is it the mainstay of our very existence, but "grub" also provides the major outlet for the efforts of powerful advertising agencies, who persuade us to buy their clients' "irresistible" and "mouth-watering" products through the press, radio and television. Thousands of millions of pounds are spent annually on commercial campaigns and food advertising is a highly specialised and sophisticated business in today's consumer age.

It was all very different before the advent of commercial television and the colourful and evocative advert (overleaf), which appeared in the match pro-gramme printed for the Scotland versus England clash at Hampden on 6 April 1935 clearly exemplifies the different style of advertising in the mid-1930s . . . style being the operative word! For the record, Scotland won that particular "Auld Enemy" confrontation 2–0, with the elegant and stylish Douglas "Dally" Duncan serving up a feast of fine football and scoring both Scottish goals. In a mood for celebrating, no doubt many of the gourmets in the 129,693 Hampden crowd galloped back to Lewis's, hung their bonnets on a hat-stand, admired the "dainty" ankles of the waitresses and tickled their discerning palates as the orchestra, recognising the significance of the occasion, almost certainly treated their emotional customers to a programme of Scottish music.

Football horizons, spiced with the international flavour of World Cup and European Championship campaigns, are infinitely wider nowadays and the "Tartan Army" have a much more varied menu from which to choose their post-match celebration meal. They could opt for a Chinese carry-out, perhaps a chicken fried-rice on days which, hopefully, are sweet for the Scots and sour for their opponents. Maybe it'll be an Indian curry, an Italian pizza, or how about the delights of a Turkish sheesh-kebab? One thing is certain . . . if any

Douglas "Dally" Duncan.

joyous Scots decide to splash out on a sit-down meal in a restaurant, they'll have a job finding an eating establishment with an orchestra and they won't satisfy their hunger for one and a tanner, will they?

It is interesting to note the extent of inflation since the great "Dally" Duncan's goals rocked the English lads back on their heels in the heyday of football over half a century ago. Today a Hampden pie costs at least ten bob (50p) and it is intriguing to observe that, partly due to the imposition of VAT on hot, take-away foods, the famished football fan of 1935 could have

Match programme advertising, 1935 vintage.

enjoyed around a dozen of Lewis's special two-bob meals for the price of a humble pie supper 1980s style! Incidentally, another advert, which appeared in that same match programme, amusingly highlights the fact that a mixture of football and whisky was an acceptable cocktail all those years ago. "Never mind the match! Bring us four 'White Label'." You certainly don't see that kind of advertising appearing in current Scottish football programmes!

Having worked on the production side of commercial television for over a quarter of a century, I have developed a keen awareness of the power of the medium and gained first-hand experience of the film and video techniques which make television such a potent and effective means of advertising and marketing products. It would be simply impossible to count the hours which I spent as a film editor "making silk purses out of sows' ears", cutting, splicing, laying music and sound-tracks, all in an effort to get the recipe right and make the ingredients visually interesting to the viewer. I remember in 1967, or thereabouts, when Celtic was the finest club side in Europe, editing the film of a Celtic versus Hibs match for Scottish Television's *Scotsport* programme. Celtic won 4–0 but could, and should, have scored around a dozen goals in what was a very one-sided affair. Being a Hibernian fan I utilised my editing skills to the full to portray the "Hibees" in the best possible light. Each time the Hibs side crossed the halfway line I hung that "attack" up on the film rack for possible inclusion in the final product. Naturally there was an unwritten obligation to include the four Celtic goals but, after much manipulation, I managed to make it appear as if the Parkhead team had broken away and scored four times, totally against the run of play and despite being subjected to constant pressure from the Easter Road men. The resultant edited "highlights" were duly transmitted and, suffice to say, the powers that be were less than happy with an end product which represented a total distortion of the truth and which brought a deluge of complaints from the Celtic faithful. Roundly criticised from all directions, I felt certain that a representative of the Post Office would shortly be calling at my door, clutching an envelope containing a couple of complimentary stand tickets for the next Hibs home match, courtesy of a very grateful Hibernian Board of Directors. However, like that impotent Hibs attack, the man with his sack of letters was posted missing and nothing dropped through the letter-box to ease my feelings of isolation or to indicate that my sterling efforts had received a stamp of approval from anyone. There has been a lot of water under my particular bridge since those far-off days and, perhaps, I'm a much more responsible individual now.

Generally speaking I share the conviction that a picture is worth a thousand words. On the other hand, as that Lewis's advert so clearly demonstrates, press and magazine advertising can also be very effective. The words are so evocative and thought-provoking that the reader is almost compelled to sample the delights on offer at the eating place.

Advertising outlets will, with the ever-increasing momentum of the technological age, change dramatically long before the advent of the twenty-first century. Satellites, cable television and the video disc will play their part in ensuring that the commercial marketeer has a much wider choice when it comes to spending the advertising budget. But what will endure is the fundamental aim of advertising, namely to sell the product in question and, in doing so, to capture the imagination of the audience or reader.

Football certainly captured the public imagination in the 1930s, because that was the decade in which Europe's biggest ever crowds packed the Hampden terracings and when attitudes to the sport were very different from what they are today. One of Scotland's greatest ever defenders, Hearts and Scotland full-back, Andy Anderson, who won twenty-three full caps between 1933 and 1939, came up with an interesting little anecdote when I visited him recently.

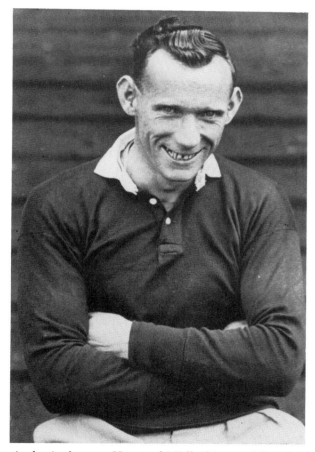

Andy Anderson, Heart of Midlothian and Scotland
. . . one of his country's greatest ever defenders.

When I was first selected to play for Scotland, in 1933, I received a letter from the SFA asking me to report at St Enoch's Hotel in Glasgow at 12.30 p.m. on the afternoon of the match. On arriving at the hotel I was introduced to "Dally" Duncan; who was the only Anglo-Scot in our side. I had never even met the Derby County player before that, yet there we were enjoying a meal in that hotel and, less than three hours later, playing together in a Scottish side which managed to beat England 2–1.

Those international team managers of today would never allow that kind of thing to happen, would they?

An example of the poetic and colourful style of writing which was so popular in the 1930s is to be found in a souvenir supplement published by the *Bulletin* newspaper to mark the Scotland versus England international played at Hampden on 28 March 1931. In my opinion the pen pictures of the Scottish team, which the anonymous scribe in the *Bulletin*'s sports' section wrote all those years ago, make much more interesting reading than the stark, factual profiles which are commonplace today. Here are the descriptions of just four of those renowned Scottish stars of yesteryear as printed in the souvenir: Johnny Thomson of Celtic, who was to die tragically just a few months later at the age of twenty-three following an accidental collision with Sam English of Rangers; Joe Nibloe, the Kilmarnock full-back who played for his country eleven times between 1929 and 1932; Davie Meiklejohn, that marvellous Rangers and Scotland captain; and George Stevenson of Motherwell, who was one of Scottish football's greatest ever inside-forwards.

J. Thomson: The latest Celt to wear the triple crown of internationalism. And it fits snugly on that so modern mop of hair. Can bend like a willow and flits from post to post with the elusiveness of a beam from a mirror on a sunny day. One hundred per cent confident about everything he does. Wellesley born and Parkhead reared. One of the few unspoilt by a football nation's platitudes.

Johnny Thomson . . . "The Prince of Goalkeepers".

Joe Nibloe.

J. Nibloe: Kilmarnock's corker of a back from Corkerhill. Another who suffers from no English complex. Of the unostentatious type until he is challenged. Then he becomes as stubborn as a mule and kicks like a bucking bronco. Has definitely made up his mind that the community singers will get no chance to warble "Poor old Joe" at the end of this day of days.

Davie Meiklejohn

D. Meiklejohn: "Who is this England?" one can imagine Dave o' Ibrox inquiring . . . must be his judicial mind. Makes himself look a very useful veteran, does this Clydebuilt Govan product who so long ago lost the accent of Maryhill Juniors. Can direct a shot that has the same effect as a broadside from a battle cruiser, but today will probably content himself with proving that he is as difficult to pass as a Hampden gateman when you haven't got a brief.

G. Stevenson: An inside-forward with a touch as light as a mother's kiss. The strategist of the Scotland attack is the stylish-moving Kilbirnie man from Motherwell. Packs a punch too, when the other fellow drops his guard, for there's lots of energy to be recognised in fifteen league goals.

George Stevenson.

Just the kind of stuff to whet the appetite of the average Scottish football fan and make him hunger for another bite at the English. Happily for the Scots, England had to swallow their pride on that spring afternoon in 1931 when, after Prime Minister Ramsay MacDonald had inspected the "troops", a Scotland side composed entirely of players based with Scottish clubs won 2–0, the goals coming from George Stevenson and the greatest goalscorer of them all . . . Jimmy McGrory of Celtic.

Hampden 1931, and Prime Minister, Ramsay MacDonald, meets the Scottish side.

That result sent shock-waves ringing round international football circles because England had been firm pre-match favourites and when the all-tartan Scottish team was chosen a huge wave of public criticism and ridicule had swamped the unfortunate players and international selection committee. Sceptical scribes in the sporting press had poured more cold water on Scotland's chances and filled their fountain pens with black ink in readiness to write Scottish international football's obituary, as well as to record the total of English goals which were certain to be piled behind the unfortunate Johnny Thomson.

The names of those "Tartan Terrors" who confounded the critics and men of little faith in 1931 are deserving of recall: *Scotland*—J. Thomson (*Celtic*); D. Blair (*Clyde*) and J. Nibloe (*Kilmarnock*); C. McNab (*Dundee*), D. Meiklejohn (*Rangers*) and J. Miller (*St Mirren*); A. Archibald (*Rangers*), G. Stevenson (*Motherwell*), J. McGrory (*Celtic*), R. McPhail (*Rangers*) and A. Morton (*Rangers*). And here are the names of the white-shirted lads who headed south with faces as red as an English rose: H. Hibbs (*Birmingham*); R. Goodall (*Huddersfield*) and E. Blenkinsop (*Sheffield Wednesday*); A. Strange (*Sheffield Wednesday*), H. Roberts (*Arsenal*) and A. Campbell (*Huddersfield*); S. Crooks (*Derby County*), G. Hodgson (*Liverpool*), W. Dean (*Everton*), H. Burgess (*Sheffield Wednesday*) and J. Crawford (*Chelsea*).

Scotland won four of the five full international matches versus England staged at Hampden in the 1930s. The 1937 clash attracted Europe's biggest ever attendance when a staggering 149,415 spectators paid £24,303 to cram the stands and the terracings at Scotland's national stadium. Outclassed and trailing 0–1 at half-time, Scotland looked a beaten side until those great inside-forwards, Tommy Walker of Hearts and Bob McPhail of Rangers, began to torment the English defence in the second half. Just two minutes after the interval centre-forward Frank O'Donnell of Preston North End equalised and Bob McPhail scored twice in the last fifteen minutes to give the Scots a 3–1 win. McPhail was smothered after each of his goals by celebrating fans who, apart from being delighted that the Scots had snatched victory from the gaping jaws of defeat, must have been thankful to gain temporary relief from what was surely a crushing experience on the terracings. A week later an estimated 20,000 supporters were locked out of Hampden when 147,365 fans (a European record for a club match) watched Celtic win the Scottish Cup for the fifteenth time by beating Aberdeen 2–1 in an enthralling final.

Unfortunately, only a few scratched and fleeting newsreel films of those historic matches exist to record the special skills of men like Tommy Walker, Bob McPhail, England's Horatio Carter and Stanley Matthews (playing in his first international versus Scotland), Matt Armstrong of Aberdeen and Celtic's match-winner, Willie Buchan. The magic of television and modern recording techniques have ensured that future generations will always be able to scrutinise and evaluate the relative talents of today's footballers . . . if only those sophisticated outside broadcast cameras could have been at Hampden Park on those two April Saturdays way back in 1937!

Two years later on 15 April 1939 . . . and thanks to the ravings of an Austrian madman called Adolf Hitler, dark war clouds were massing menacingly across the continent of Europe. Against this spine-chilling backdrop of impending tragedy, Scotland only required to draw and England needed

Homeward bound . . . a vast Hampden crowd of the late 1930s.

a victory to win the British International Championship at a rain-drenched Hampden. With just three minutes left for play and the score standing at 1–1, it looked as if the Scots had done enough to be crowned champions. But, as John MacAdam of the *Daily Express* described in his match report, the real drama was about to unfold:

> Matthews gets the ball and tears inside. On the run he hits it with his right foot true and hard for the far corner of the net. Jerry Dawson leaps for it, fists it round the corner of the post. Corner, and the ball is badly cleared. Goulden gets it, swings it to Matthews . . . Matthews has it in marvellous control and the roar is a tornado of sound now. Matthews belts it right across as true as an arrow to Tom Lawton's head. Lawton crashes it into the net and the game is won . . . and lost!

So England won the "big international" for the first time since 1934 and recorded their solitary Hampden win in the Thirties.

Many years later (when manager of Liverpool), Preston's Bill Shankly who in the right-half position had grafted tirelessly for Scotland's cause, described his personal recollection of Lawton's historic goal:

> I sensed danger and moved to try and prevent Stan from crossing . . . but I was far too late. As the ball sailed over my head I turned to see Lawton run in, throw his neck back and lash the ball into the roof of the net with his head. I'll never forget the sound that ball made as it hit the rain-sodden rigging, ran down the back of the net in a spray of water and was buried behind our goalkeeper, Jerry Dawson. Lawton was a great player . . . a really great player!

Incidentally, Tommy Lawton's Everton team-mate, Joe Mercer, was playing in only his second full international match and, from all accounts, the young left-half turned in a top-class performance: "Mercer was magnificent all through, even in the first half, when it looked as if Scotland were going to have a runaway win," wrote John MacAdam. "He was back in defence, first on one side then on the other, always fishing the ball from a danger spot and pushing it through to his own forwards."

Naturally, those rain clouds were edged with a silver lining as far as the English were concerned. But there was also an ironical twist attached to the fact that England had turned on the style in that match-winning second period. The ground conditions were so dreadful that both teams completely changed their strip at half-time and the "Sassenachs" re-emerged clad in shirts borrowed from their Hampden hosts, Queen's Park. True to their tremendous and long-standing traditions of sportsmanship, Scotland's

The great Tommy Lawton.

mother club had shown compassion to the "enemy" and, in doing so, had played a small, but perhaps significant, part in contributing to Scotland's downfall. Here are the names of the "Pride of England" who dampened Scottish spirits at a rainswept Hampden on that April Saturday in 1939: Woodley (*Chelsea*); Morris (*Wolverhampton Wanderers*) and Hapgood (*Arsenal*); Willingham (*Huddersfield Town*), Cullis (*Wolverhampton Wanderers*) and Mercer (*Everton*); Matthews (*Stoke City*), Hall (*Tottenham Hotspur*), Lawton (*Everton*), Goulden (*West Ham United*) and Beasley (*Huddersfield Town*). And, just for the record . . . the disappointed Scottish team: Dawson (*Rangers*); Carabine (*Third Lanark*) and Cummings (*Aston Villa*); Shankly

(*Preston North End*), Baxter (*Middlesbrough*) and McNab (*West Bromwich Albion*); McSpadyen (*Partick Thistle*), Walker (*Hearts*), Dougal (*Preston North End*), Venters (*Rangers*) and Milne (*Middlesbrough*).

The last hundred years have been the most eventful in the story of mankind, with one significant invention and scientific discovery coming hard on the heels of another.

The great Joe Mercer.

In 1876, Queen's Park beat Third Lanark 2–0 in a replay to win the Scottish Cup for the third time. Despite the concerted efforts of Quintin Hogg and The Honourable Arthur Fitzgerald Kinnaird, Old Etonians were beaten 3–0 by the Wanderers in a replay of the fifth FA Cup Final. And a Scot, Alexander Graham Bell, invented and patented the telephone!

Exactly half a century later, in 1926, the town of Paisley first savoured the sweet taste of victory in a Scottish Cup Final when St Mirren defeated Celtic 2–0 at Hampden. Bolton Wanderers beat Manchester City 1–0 in the FA Cup

Bolton Wanderers, FA Cup winners 1926. Players only, back row left to right: Haworth, Nuttall, Pym, Jennings and Greenhalgh. Front row: Butler, Jack, J.R. Smith, Joe Smith, Vizard and Seddon.

Final at Wembley while, back at Burnden Park in Bolton, 10,000 spectators at a Central League fixture against Huddersfield Town burst into rapturous joy on hearing the Marconiphone announcement that, with less than fifteen minutes left for play, David Jack had scored the Wanderers' goal at the Empire Stadium. And another Scot, John Logie Baird, invented television!

Yes, Man's ability to communicate more easily with his fellows owes much to Scottish ingenuity and has advanced beyond comprehension since, in the 1870s, an eager and impatient Sports Editor in a Glasgow newspaper office had to await the arrival of carrier-pigeons winging their way back to that office with some far-flung journalist's match report, before the presses could roll and the man in the street could find out how the likes of Renton and Vale of Leven had fared in the Scottish Cup!

Nobody can possibly predict the effect which those rapidly advancing frontiers of science and technology will have on the soccer scene over the next few hundred years. Who knows . . . perhaps football's version of *The War of the Worlds* will be waged across distant galaxies as Earthmen attempt to outplay creatures from, as yet, undiscovered planets. Maybe, 20,000 years from now, when our present civilisation is long gone, some eminent archaeologist of the time will unearth those great stadiums at Hampden and Wembley; mind-boggling finds which will create as much public interest then as the discovery by archaeologist Howard Carter (not Horatio Carter) of the tomb of Egypt's boy Pharaoh, Tutankhamun, did in 1922 and will also attract the huge number of tourists which the Colosseum in that "Eternal City" of Rome does today. And, as those future men painstakingly sift their way through the dust of ages, perhaps they'll stumble across priceless treasures like the Scottish and FA Cups on which are engraved the names of weird and long gone towns such as Bury and Falkirk. Maybe they'll gaze in wonder and total bewilderment at "manuscripts" called match programmes, containing unusual words such as "throw-in" and "off side" as well as strange sounding names of twentieth-century gladiators like "Dixie" Dean, Charlie Nicholas and "Butch" Wilkins. When awe-struck historians of the twenty-second century cast their disbelieving eyes over the records and statistics of soccer, they'll surely find it incredible that, in season 2089–90, little Albion Rovers won the European Cup, Crewe Alexandra beat Liverpool 5–0 in the FA Cup Final and Malta were World Cup winners for the fourth consecutive time, after hammering Luxembourg 6–2 in a Peking final. Those men could even unlock the secrets of the "attic fanatic's" den and wonder just how one of their distant ancestors could become so obsessed with this ancient ball game called soccer. Who can tell . . . those future beings may even unearth football's most famous edifice, the Hampden pie-and-Bovril stall! Doubtless, they will recoil in horror and total revulsion when their food analysts divulge the contents of the twentieth-century football fan's staple diet!

However, all of that is light years away and, admittedly, just a little bit far-fetched. But although the future of football is shrouded in a cloak of uncertainty, there is no doubt whatsoever that the world of soccer was very different in bygone days and that the game itself has changed almost out of recognition since, in 1862, Notts County became the first of Britain's current senior clubs to be founded and Queen's Park set the ball rolling north of the border in 1867.

Was it, though, a much more enjoyable and palatable game in the 1930s or 1950s, when huge crowds were attracted to the terracings? Or is the

Fans queue for tickets for the 1954 Celtic v Aberdeen Scottish Cup final.

fast-food diet of soccer being dished out today more likely to titillate the taste buds of the average fan? Nobody can possibly come up with the definitive answer to those questions, can they? Nor can anyone remotely begin to predict the long-term future of the game or start to imagine just how wide old football's horizons could become:

> I wonder if, one day, they'll play,
> The fitba' on the Moon.
> If Martians will, to beat old Earth,
> Their finest team send doon.
> If our grand lads, in days to come,
> Their talents will display,
> On planets in the far beyond,
> Across the Milky Way.
>
> Perhaps, my friends, in times ahead,
> Our fans will travel far,
> To watch that wee team which they love,
> On some bright, distant star.
> Maybe they'll see those heroes play,
> In some new-fangled pattern,
> . . . Beat Venus, Pluto and old Mars,
> . . . And run more rings round Saturn!

Who knows! But of one thing we can be certain . . . this wonderful old ball game will always provide a veritable banquet of food for thought!

8

THE MAN WITH THE DANCING EYES

Jericho House is a building of some substance. It stands little more than a stone's throw from Glasgow Airport. The busy M8 motorway is only yards away and the floodlights in St Mirren's ground can be seen on the Paisley skyline. From his window in the old folk's home, eighty-year-old Patsy Gallacher looks out over football pitches where he played as a lad. He watches the planes flying in and out of Scotland's busiest airport and recalls with great affection and emotion the days when, as a Sunderland inside-forward, he was one of the "darlings" of Roker Park. This friendly old man, who scored many vital goals for the Wearside club in the 1930s, has tears welling in his eyes as he gazes at a picture of himself in that so famous red and white jersey.

Way back in 1927, when he left his native Bridge of Weir in Renfrewshire to join the Sunderland ground staff, the seventeen-year-old could never have imagined that he was destined to spend eleven very happy years in the football-mad North-East of England. Patsy didn't know then that, in season 1935–36,

Patsy, aged eighty, on one of those pitches where he played as a lad.

he would figure prominently in a League Championship winning side. Nor would the inside-forward ever have believed that he was to collect an FA Cup winner's medal in 1937 following an epic and historic Sunderland victory over Preston North End.

Gallacher played with and against almost all the great football names of his generation. How he remembers team-mates Bobby Gurney, Raich Carter and later, when he joined Stoke City in November 1938, Stanley Matthews. How proud he was to line up alongside that marvellous Glasgow Rangers' goalkeeper, Jerry Dawson, and Roker Park team-mate, Jimmy Connor, when, in the dark blue of his country, he gained his only cap against Northern Ireland in

Patsy Gallacher . . .
Sunderland and Scotland.
"The Man with the Dancing Eyes".

Belfast in 1934 and scored Scotland's solitary goal in a 2-1 defeat. How Gallacher enjoyed the tremendous battles with the mighty Arsenal side of the 1930s. It was a privilege, indeed, to play against stars of the calibre of Cliff Bastin, Ted Drake and Alex James . . . and memories of the incomparable Bill Shankly of "Proud Preston" are very dear to Patsy.

All of that is a far cry from Gallacher's early days when, in the back court of his Ladebank Terrace home in Bridge of Weir, he and his pals played football at every given opportunity on a "pitch" lined with sawdust, kindly supplied by their principal sponsor . . . the local joiner! "We played with a clootie ba' in those days," says Patsy, adding, "For those who don't know, a clootie ba' is simply some old rags rolled up into a ball and tied tightly with string . . . we just couldn't afford to buy the real thing."

Like many lads of his age, young Gallacher just lived for the game and had little or no time for such mundane pastimes as chatting up those "daft" girls or sitting bored out of his mind in the front stalls of the nearest cinema. "Football meant absolutely everything to me," he says. "I remember when a pupil at St Mirin's Academy in Paisley being told by Mr McCabe, my history teacher, that if I didn't stop talking and thinking about nothing other than kicking a ball and concentrate on passing my exams, he would make it his business to see that I was dropped from the school team. I failed those exams and, for a short spell, someone else took my place in the first eleven."

But that suspension represented only a temporary set-back because, on leaving school, the skinny and skilful inside-forward played for his local side, Bridge of Weir Thistles as well as Linwood St Colville's, and within a very short space of time became a magnet which attracted the attention of many of the country's top scouts. The youngster and, more importantly, his father were eventually persuaded that the lad's football future lay in Sunderland. So young Gallacher left the sleepily rural atmosphere of his country village and excitedly, yet a little apprehensively, headed for the soccer-daft North-East of England.

Sunderland was a busy old place at that time, with as much as five million tons of coal being shipped annually from a Wearside town which also boasted eight thriving shipyards and, justifiably, laid claim to being one of the most important shipbuilding centres in the world. When our old pal, Tommy McInally, joined Sunderland in 1928 and assumed the role of club captain, the ex-Celtic star was happy to take the fledgeling footballer under his wing.

"Tommy, who had been one of my boyhood heroes, would have been an earth-shattering success on the stage because he was a real comedian and a marvellous character," says Gallacher. "In September 1928, almost a year after my arrival at Roker Park, I remember telling Tommy that Sunderland had asked me to sign a full professional contract with the club and that I intended to comply with their wishes." With a broad grin on his face Patsy continued: "To my utter astonishment Tommy shouted aloud 'Sign for Sunderland . . . don't be so bloody stupid son . . . haven't I told you that Celtic are dead keen to get you . . . and that's a fact.' That outburst landed Tommy in hot water," adds Gallacher. "His words were overheard by Sunderland's chief scout, Sammy Blyth, and naturally, when McInally was reported, he was hauled over the proverbial coals by club officials less than happy with the fact that their club captain was desperately trying to persuade me to sign for another team."

Tommy McInally's passionate plea had fallen on deaf ears because the youthful Gallacher was having a whale of a time at Roker and had made up his mind to sign for the English First Division giants . . . a decision which he was never to regret. By the early 1930s the lad from Bridge of Weir had served his apprenticeship and his ball-playing skills, goal-scoring flair and heading ability soon earned him a regular spot in the Sunderland first team.

English football was dominated by Herbert Chapman's mighty Arsenal side in those days. The "Gunners" were virtually unstoppable in the annual championship race and, clearly, it was going to prove a monumental task for any side to wrest the title from the London club's grasp. By the time season 1935–36 kicked off, Arsenal, who had topped the League in the previous three seasons, were firm favourites to make it four Championship successes in a row. But those ''Gunners'' were forced to surrender to a Roker Park side which leapt to the front of the pack and, firing on all cylinders, clinched the League flag with a 7–2 win at Birmingham on Easter Monday 1936. Sunderland, with Gallacher playing a starring role, banged in twenty more goals than any other side and won the Championship by a staggering eight-point margin. Amazingly, the Wearsiders scored 109 League goals during that

Sunderland FC. First Division Champions, 1935–36. Back row, left to right: H. Carter, C. Thomson, A. Hall, J. Mapson, A. Hasting (captain), G. Collins, J. Clarke. Front left to right: J. Cochrane (manager), R. Davis, R. Gurney, P. Gallacher, J. Connor and A. Reid (trainer).

glorious winning campaign while, on the other side of the coin, the defence lost seventy-four . . . the highest number of goals ever conceded by First Division Champions. Small wonder, then, that many years later Bill Shankly described the Sunderland forward line of Bert Davis, Raich Carter, Bobby Gurney, Patsy Gallacher and Jimmy Connor as the greatest he had ever seen.

That title win was Sunderland's sixth and meant that they then shared with Aston Villa the distinction of having been League Champions more often than any other side. However, despite their Grade 'A' Championship pedigree, the coveted FA Cup had always eluded the Wearsiders.

Season 1936–37, and the draw for the third round of the competition sent the Rokerites off on the long journey to The Dell in Southampton, where the match attracted a record crowd and Sunderland won 3–2. Fortune certainly smiled on the lads from the North East in the next round at Luton when, after being given the run-around in the first forty-five minutes and going in at the interval fortunate to be only 2–0 down, heavy, black clouds suddenly burst open . . . torrential rain ensured that the playing surface "took a stud" more easily in the second half and ground conditions were much more suited to the ball-playing skills of Gallacher and his mates, who managed to salvage a 2–2 draw.

Press headlines announcing Sunderland's 3–1 replay victory were relegated to second billing by the news from "down under" that the great Don Bradman had scored a double century for Australia in the second innings of the fourth Test match, before being caught and bowled by England's Walter Hammond when his score stood at 212 runs.

Sunderland's fifth-round opponents were Swansea, who travelled to Roker Park after winning a replay at York and, despite receiving tremendous vocal support from their noisy and flamboyant fans who banged frying pans together and tied leeks to the goalposts, were predictably beaten with consumate ease. The Welsh lads headed back to the "Land of Their Fathers" having lost by three goals to nil.

On 6 March 1937 front-page headlines chronicled the bloody events of the Spanish Civil War, while the fearsome prospect of a quarter-final tie with Wolves at Molineux, stood between the Wearside boys and a place in the FA Cup semi-finals. A record 57,751 fans watched the match which ended 1–1 and, with those twin towers of Wembley looming ever larger, the winners were drawn to meet Third Division Millwall in the semi-final. On the other side of the world Australia became the first cricketing country to win a Test series 3–2 after having lost the first two matches while, more importantly, back on that Wembley trail, 61,796 fans filed through the turnstiles at Roker for the Wednesday afternoon replay with Wolves. The home supporters were shattered when, with only four minutes of the match remaining, Galley broke the deadlock and scored for the visitors. However, thirty seconds from time, amid scenes of great relief and jubilation, Bobby Gurney scored a spectacular goal to level the match. Len Duns put Sunderland ahead in extra-time but Wolves equalised through Thompson. The two First Division giants headed for

Hillsborough in Sheffield on the following Monday for the next instalment of an epic tie. By this time Sunderland had decided that enough was enough and, in front of a crowd numbering almost 50,000, romped to a convincing 4–0 win.

Semi-final opponents, Millwall, were the first Third Division outfit ever to reach that stage of the competition and had beaten First Division sides in the last three of their six ties, including an historic 2–0 sixth-round victory over League leaders and eventual champions, Manchester City. There was clearly no room for complacency in the Roker ranks when that crucial match was staged at Huddersfield in April 1937, a fact which was strikingly underlined when the London side took a tenth minute lead through a fine goal from their player/manager, Dave Mangnall. However, Gurney equalised before the break and in the sixty-fifth minute a wonderful headed goal from Gallacher ensured that Sunderland were Wembley-bound and set for a May Day FA Cup Final shoot-out with Lancashire big guns, Preston North End.

"My match-winning header against Millwall was the greatest and most important goal I ever scored," says Gallacher. That spectacular winner set the huge contingent of Wearside fans wild with joy and, when the final whistle blew, the Sunderland faithful in the gigantic crowd of 62,813 poured on to the field from the jam-packed terraces, lifted Gallacher shoulder-high and carried their hero of the hour all the way to the dressing-room. Later, amid scenes of sheer delirium, Patsy was raised on high once again and transported to the Sunderland-bound train by hordes of cheering and overjoyed supporters. "The scenes were beyond belief," says Gallacher. "But, amazing though it may seem, the real celebrations were still to come. . . . I was sitting playing cards with my team-mates, when two policemen boarded the train at Durham and told us that the streets of Sunderland were choked with happy fans, while a huge crowd chanting my name was at the town's station awaiting the arrival of our train. Plans had apparently been laid to ensure my safe passage through the 'mob' . . . so I sat back wondering just what lay ahead of me."

The welcome which those conquering heroes, and in particular Patsy Gallacher, received on their arrival in Sunderland was way beyond their wildest expectations. "A mass of bodies surged on to the platform when the train pulled in," says Gallacher, with a twinkle in his eye and clearly revelling in the chance to recall those marvellous events of over half a century ago. "All of the players were mobbed and the police could do little about it," he said, adding: "But it was me they were really after. Before I knew what was happening I was tossed into the air and found myself being transported along on a sea of red and white. The rest of the lads had managed to make their get-away in a fleet of taxis . . . but there was no hiding place for me."

On an ever-swelling tide of emotion, that great wave of joyous humanity carried the bobbing and astonished figure that was Patsy Gallacher the 150 yards to the entrance of the Grand Hotel, before he was finally swept from the mayhem and turbulence and washed ashore on to an island of comparative sanity within the portals of the hotel. "I was trapped in that building for hours while those marvellous fans continued to shout my name. . . . Not only were they fantastic fans, but they were the nicest folk imaginable. While being carried from the station I lost a very special wrist-watch, which had been presented to me by the club to commemorate our 1935–36 Championship win. I never really expected to see it again, but should have known better. Because, on the Monday morning an unknown fan, who had found it, handed the watch in to the ground," recalled Patsy, before adding: "To look at me now, Jim, you must find all of that a little hard to believe. . . . You can't imagine these stiff, old legs and this head of white hair scoring piles of goals in the 1930s, can you, son? Look up the record books and you will also be amazed to discover how many hat-tricks I scored against top-class opposition."

The old boy is now in his element. His natural modesty has temporarily deserted him and those eyes of his dance as he eagerly grabs a rare opportunity to bend a highly willing and very interested ear. Managing to interrupt the flow of unashamed nostalgia, I asked how he felt the top players in his day stood in comparison with their modern counterparts. "None of today's players are even remotely in the same league as Alex James. He was the greatest of them all," said Gallacher emphatically. "The man was an absolute genius and the complete master of the ball. Alex's positional sense and passing skills had to be seen to be believed . . . you would know what football is all about had you seen him play. The modern players are certainly faster and fitter than we were but they just aren't in the same class when it comes to skill and the ability to entertain the paying public," adds Patsy, recalling another football great. "Ireland's Peter Doherty was another absolutely outstanding player. Peter's ball control, balance and ability to read a game were out of this world. He was the complete footballer as well as one of the nicest guys you could ever hope to meet. No wonder they called him "Peter the Great".

But back to Sunderland Football Club and that head-to-head with mighty Preston in the 1937 FA Cup Final. "On the day of the match, as our team

Alex James in his Arsenal days.

bus made its way through the streets of the capital from our Bushey Hall Hotel base in Watford, heading towards Wembley, we were absolutely astounded by the sheer numbers of fans from the North East who had turned those streets of London into a blazing carnival of red and white,'' recalled the former Sunderland star. ''Our team spirit was terrific and it was a happy bunch of lads who sat and enjoyed the singsong which was customary when we were en route to any away match. Goalkeeper, Johnny Mapson, was a great George Formby fan and, for the umpteenth time, sang *When I'm Cleaning Windows* as the coach rolled ever nearer to the Empire Stadium. I was asked to sing *Danny Boy* because ours had been a rocky road to the final and the lads felt that, if I sang that particular song, as I had done before each round, our good luck might just stay with us for a further ninety minutes . . . so, naturally, I obliged. Then left-half, Sandy McNab, who won his first cap for Scotland in the same year, suggested that we should all sing *Abide With Me*. Picture the scene. It was the biggest day of our lives, we were only yards from the stadium and, as the police escort of six motor-bikes guided us through the thronging and cheering crowds with the Roker fans waving their huge red and white banners proudly proclaiming *Sunderland For the Cup* and *H-away the Lads*, to a man we sang that wonderful hymn at the top of our voices.''

Sunderland manager, Johnny Cochrane, and trainer, Andy Reid, were no strangers to the special atmosphere engendered by a national cup final. Eleven years earlier, in 1926, the duo had steered St Mirren to a 2–0 win over Celtic at Hampden . . . and that fine club's first ever Scottish Cup victory. Would they achieve a remarkable double and guide Sunderland to a first FA Cup triumph?

Fresh from a 2–1 victory over Aberdeen in the 1937 Scottish Cup Final, the victorious Celtic team were at Wembley to lend support to their former team-mates, the brothers Hugh and Frank O'Donnell, who were both included in the Preston line-up. ''Among the first people we met at the stadium were the Celtic lads,'' recalls Gallacher. ''They were wearing blue and white rosettes of all things. How about that? The Celts proudly wearing the colours of their great rivals, Glasgow Rangers . . . bet that hasn't happened before or since,'' said the old boy, sporting a broad grin and adding: ''I teased the life out of Jimmy McGrory, asking him what they thought they were playing at coming down to Wembley and being crazy enough to support a lost cause like Preston.'' To which the Celtic and Scotland centre-forward replied: ''Time will tell, Patsy, time will tell . . . but it should be quite a match.''

1937 was Coronation year and both George VI and Queen Elizabeth were present at what was to prove an historic occasion . . . historic, too, because that was the first FA Cup final of which any part was televised!

For the fourth time in five ties Sunderland found themselves a goal down when centre-forward, Frank O'Donnell, slotted home a well-worked goal in the thirty-eighth minute, to the sheer delight of Preston fans and that Celtic contingent with their blue and white ribbons. Frank O'Donnell had scored in every round and that goal was his eleventh of the competition. Even at that early stage it looked as if pre-match betting that Frank would prove to be the Preston match-winner when the chips were down was very much on the cards. However, early in the second half, Sunderland's left-winger, Eddie Burbanks, forced a corner, took the kick himself, and his perfectly flighted cross was headed on to Gurney, who grabbed the equaliser with a characteristic backward header. With seventy-two minutes on the clock a wonder goal from Horatio Carter put the Wearsiders in front and, six minutes later, Burbanks added a third following a tremendous defence splitting pass from Gallacher. So Horatio Stratton Carter, Sunderland born and bred and married in Derby only a matter of days earlier with Gurney his best

The Sunderland lads celebrate by lifting captain Horatio Carter and that famous cup on high. Gallacher is half hidden behind the London "bobby".

man, gaily pranced up those famous Wembley steps, proudly accepted the trophy from Queen Elizabeth and became the first Sunderland captain to raise an FA Cup on high since the club was founded fifty-eight years earlier in 1879. In the early 1900s a gypsy woman, on reading the palm of a Sunderland player, predicted that his club would never win the competition until a Scotswoman sat on the throne. Sunderland had regularly flattered to deceive until 1937 . . . when Scottish-born Queen Elizabeth, wife of King George VI and mother of our present Queen, more than fulfilled the gypsy's prophecy when she actually handed the cup to Carter.

Interestingly, in 1913 Sunderland had taken a crate of beer to London and a final. Beaten 1–0 by Aston Villa at Crystal Palace, the Wearsiders swore that the beer would remain unopened until they won the FA Cup. Here is the Sunderland line-up which poured that aged ale down their throats and succeeded where so many illustrious predecessors had failed: Mapson; Gorman and Hall; Thomson, Johnston and McNab; Duns, Carter, Gurney, Gallacher and Burbanks. And those disappointed laddies from Lancashire, Preston North End—Burns, Gallimore and Beattie, Shankly, Tremelling and Milne; Dougal, Beresford, F. O'Donnell, Fagan and H.O'Donnell. I wonder if those Celtic lads stayed on to watch the presentation of the trophy!

On the Monday evening following that historic victory, the town of Sunderland was brought to a standstill once again as everyone from babes in arms to the next door neighbour's granny painted the town red and gave the home-coming Wembley heroes an ecstatic Wearside welcome.

But what a stark contrast the following season! There were no crowds to welcome the Sunderland party at that same railway station in the wake of a 3–1 FA Cup semi-final defeat by Huddersfield Town at Blackburn. "Roker Park was like a mortuary and all the talk was of war," says Gallacher. "My Sunderland days were virtually over because, later in 1938, Stoke City manager, Bob McGrory, who came from Bishopton near my home village of Bridge of Weir, travelled up to Roker and took me back with him to the Potteries. For me, things were never really quite the same again. Football, like life itself, is a yo-yo of ups and downs, isn't it, Jim? The days which I spent with those wonderful down-to-earth folk in Sunderland were the happiest days of my life," says Patsy, adding: "I'm still as daft about football as I was when our back-door Celtic and back-door Rangers drew 35–35 playing with that 'clootie 'ba' way back in the early 1920s. Ladebank Terrace, the joiner's shop and most of my mates are now long gone, but, when that old head of mine hits the pillow at night, I'm still kicking the sheets, dribbling, scoring and cheering . . . dreaming of those days when I was privileged to play in the Sunderland forward line."

In common with so many of the great front runners of his day, Gallacher's legs are now riddled with arthritis. It is, quite simply, the penalty he has to pay for all those years of dedication on the football field. Merely an inevitable, if unwelcome, legacy from the uncompromising clashes with those great defenders of the 1930s. Patsy bears the considerable and constant pain in characteristic fashion, secure in the knowledge that, given his time over again, he wouldn't change a thing.

Before he died, in May 1980, Patsy Gallacher's Sunderland and Scotland team-mate, Jimmy Connor, described his former left-wing partner as, "A guy who displayed real style both on and off the football field. Paddy was a very natty dresser, who often wore pin-striped suits and spats. He was also a man who would give you anything when he had it . . . we used to call him Sir Patrick Gallacher."

The dedicated follower of fashion's stylish play was generally praised by the country's top football names. As already mentioned, Patsy Gallacher has always had the utmost respect for that highly talented and much revered Irish inside-forward, Peter Doherty, a respect which is, to this day, reciprocated by Doherty. "Paddy, as many of his fellow professionals called him, was the perfect example of a natural ball player," says Peter. "As far as I am concerned the man was a footballing great whose name should never die. Gallacher's talents brought him few rewards. His tremendous contribution to the game was never properly recognised."

Joe Mercer, who earned universal praise both as a player and as a manager, is one of the best loved and most respected figures in the history of the sport. Joe, who describes Gallacher as "a magnificent player", came up with one of the best football anecdotes I have ever heard when I asked if he had any specific recollections of playing against the Sunderland inside-forward. "I can never forget one occasion in the late 1930s," says Mercer. "I lined up in the Everton half-back line against Sunderland at Goodison Park and Gallacher was directly opposed to me. In the first half Paddy gave me a terrible roasting . . . in fact he absolutely destroyed me in front of a crowd of almost 70,000," admits the former Everton, Arsenal and England star. "I could do absolutely nothing with him as he turned me this way and that, pulled me out of position, ghosted past me and made me feel utterly foolish. The half-time whistle came as a great relief and I sat, head in hands, in the dressing-room wondering just what I could do to contain the man. I came to the conclusion that I was giving him far too much space and that I would have to add a bit of steel to my tackles. From the start of the second half I stuck to the Sunderland man like a leech and generally made things tougher for him. Midway through that second period, Paddy, who was coming through with the ball, noticed that I was set to come in with another hard tackle. To my utter astonishment Gallacher stopped dead in his tracks, held up his hand and said, 'Joe son . . . if you want the ball that much you can have it' and with that he rolled the ball to my feet while the huge crowd watched totally bewildered. I accepted the gesture and played on . . . but I did so with a deep sense of shame.''

That gem of a story represents the ultimate tribute to Gallacher. But it also speaks volumes for the great Joe Mercer. How many men in football, or any other walk of life for that matter, would be big and honest enough to heap such praise on a rival at their own expense?

There was, of course, another famous footballer who answered to the name of Patsy Gallagher (with a ''g''). Irish internationalist, Patsy Gallagher of Celtic was a frail looking figure of a man who stood five feet six inches tall and weighed in at only seven and a half stone when he first appeared in the Glasgow club's famous green and white hooped jersey. Gallagher played for

Patsy Gallagher . . . Glasgow Celtic and Ireland.

Celtic and Falkirk between seasons 1911-12 and 1931-32 and, despite his diminutive stature, will go down as one of the most talented forwards in the history of the game. ''The Mighty Atom'', as Gallagher was so aptly nicknamed, won four Scottish Cup winner's badges and seven League

Championship medals with Celtic. From time to time there has been a certain amount of confusion as to how the Celtic legend's name should be spelt. So should a "c" or a "g" be included in his surname? Patsy's son, Tommy, a fine player in his own right, who played for Dundee and the Scottish League not long after the war, explains: "My father was only three years old when the Gallaghers arrived in Scotland from Ireland in the 1890s," says Tommy. "Those members of the family who were educated in Ireland spelt their surname with a 'g'. But, on arrival in Clydebank, a joiner mistakenly screwed a nameplate which was spelt with a 'c' on to the house door and the family left it, finding it simpler to adopt the Scottish spelling." So, despite the fact that Celtic's Patsy signed those famous autographs Patsy Gallacher, the truth of the matter is that, although either spelling is acceptable, the surname on his birth certificate reads Gallagher!

It is highly probable that Sunderland's version of a top-class inside-forward with the initials P.G. would have won many more medals had the comical, yet highly talented, Tommy McInally managed to persuade him to ditch Sunderland and sign for Glasgow Celtic. There is no disputing the fact that in Scotland a regular spot in the Rangers or Celtic first team has always brought with it a guaranteed haul of medals for the player . . . whatever his talents! Not so in England, because, even with a certain amount of reluctance, the most ardent of Scottish football fans would be forced to concede that the FA Cup competition is the greatest and most openly contested cup tournament in the world. On the other hand, football enthusiasts south of the border must agree that the high standard of competition, both in the FA Cup and Football League, has always owed a great deal to the contribution and influence of the Scots. For instance, Sunderland fielded five Scotsmen in their 1937 Cup final side, while Preston, whose Secretary/Manager, Tommy Muirhead, was a famous Rangers and Scotland star, had no fewer than seven Scots in their defeated line-up! In 1973, when the Wearsiders, then in the Second Division, surprised everyone with their 1–0 FA Cup final victory over ex-Sunderland captain Don Revie's red-hot favourites, Leeds United, Scottish import, Ian Porterfield, was the player who grabbed the all-important match-winning goal. Indeed it was a Scot, James Allan, who was instrumental in the founding of Sunderland Football Club in 1879!

Incidentally, Sunderland's greatest rivals, Newcastle United, hold the record in England for fielding a side which contained most Scotsmen. On 6 October 1928, they beat Leeds United 3–2 and only centre-half, Edmund Wood, was not Scottish-born. And, while on the subject, it is worth noting that William McGregor from Perthshire was the brains behind, and instigator of, the formation of the Football League in 1888!

Rules for Training.

7 30 a.m. — Rise, half-an-hour's stroll.

8 30 „ — Breakfast, weak tea, chops, eggs, dry toast or stale bread.

9 45 „ — Exercise, bath to follow.

1 0 p.m — Dinner of plain roast or boiled joints of mutton or beef, with an occasional fowl, fresh vegetables, rice or tapioca puddings, stale bread, a glass of beer or claret.

3 30 „ — Exercise.

5 30 „ — Tea, fresh fish, light boiled eggs, or chops.

7 30 „ — An hour's stroll.

9 0 „ — Supper, glass of beer or claret and bread.

10 0 „ — Retire to bed.

N.B. — Butter, sugar, milk, potatoes, and tobacco must be sparingly used.

When out walking the whole of the players must keep together and accompany the trainer. This rule must be observed.

The orders of the trainer must be strictly obeyed. Any player who neglects to comply with the above rules will be reported and dealt with as the Committee think fit.

By Order of the Directors.

Sunderland's training schedule 1890s style!

"I certainly never regretted the fact that I played all my senior football in England," says Patsy Gallacher, "although it still irks me that Sunderland's Scottish manager, Johnny Cochrane, more than once refused to release me for international duty because of the pressures and commitments at Roker. Ironically, had Sunderland been less successful, I might have won more caps."

Then, with a sudden change of mood, Patsy started laughing and, handing me a copy of Sunderland's centenary brochure, said, "I'm glad that I didn't play for the club in the 1890s." Intrigued, I asked him what he meant. "Because, in those days, the players had to eat stale bread and be in bed by ten o'clock . . . and that certainly wouldn't have suited me! Have a look at page seventeen and you'll see what I'm talking about." Turning to the appropriate page I found Sunderland's *Rules of Training* in the year 1897 (below). A strict timetable and code of conduct with stale bread on the menu! I wonder why they didn't insist on a cold bath before breakfast!

Always game for a laugh, Patsy Gallacher is as Scottish as haggis. But the white-haired old man, who simply oozes character and personality, has left a large part of his big heart on Wearside. Who knows? Maybe one of those wee Paisley boys who play football just outside Patsy's window will, one day, end up at Roker. And who can tell . . . that may just signal the rebirth of the glory days for Sunderland Football Club! That would be a prospect which would thrill a contented and delightful old man who has an abiding love for the club and who, over five decades ago, was the "darling" of the "greatest football fans on Earth".

Till the day I die I will never forget Gallacher and those dancing, glinting eyes of his. He talks about the game like no other man I have ever met. To listen to his sparkling gems of football wisdom born of years of first-hand experience is indeed a privilege. Many of the happiest hours of my life have been spent in his engrossing and uplifting company.

I am reminded of the final scene in the musical *Camelot*, which is one of my favourite movies. King Arthur (alias actor Richard Harris) discovers a young lad called Tom, aged about fourteen, hiding behind the lines before a battle. When the king asks the boy what he is doing in such a place and at such a time, the lad tells Arthur that he has come to fight on the side of justice and freedom for all because he has heard all about the tales of *The Knights of the Round Table* and of their heroic deeds. After taking his sword, Excalibur, and knighting the boy Sir Tom of Warwick, Arthur tells the youngster to run behind the lines, to live, to grow up, to grow old and to forget about fighting in the battle. Could it be significant, as I am reliably informed by one who moves in such exalted circles, that there are precious few round tables to be found in the boardrooms of our football clubs? But I really must end this chapter on a positive and less cynical note . . . with King Arthur's words to a henchman who enquires as to the lad's identity and asks Arthur what he is doing talking to a boy when he has a battle to fight. ''I've won my battle and here is my victory,'' replies the king, hugging Tom. ''What we did will be remembered. You'll see.''

Gallacher, like Arthur in the legend of *Camelot*, has experienced the high points and the low points in a life which has been laced with both glory and tragedy. But somehow the king's words in that film seem to best express my sentiments when I think of my dear old friend, Patsy Gallacher. ''Who was that?'' asks the henchman. ''One of what we all are,'' replies the king. ''Less than a drop in the great blue motion of the sunlit sea, but it seems that some of the drops sparkle . . . some of them really do sparkle!''

9

GEORGE CUMMINGS . . . SUPERSTAR!

George Cummings . . . superstar!

A moulder in a Stirlingshire iron foundry before embarking on a senior football career, the late George Cummings was, himself, cast in the defensive mould of the immaculate Walter Arnott. One of the world of soccer's greatest ever defenders, the left-back was already a Scottish internationalist when he joined Aston Villa from Partick Thistle on 13 November 1935. Villa paid the Glasgow club the then staggering sum of £9,500 for the transfer of their star player and, even at that price, George proved to be a real bargain buy.

Like Arnott, Cummings was a footballing "giant amongst giants" and, for almost two decades, was outstanding in the golden age of football when wonderful players were plentiful and Britain's biggest ever crowds flocked to the terracings. Supremely confident in his own ability, two-footed and a complete master of his craft with skills which complemented a fine physique, he endeared himself to the fans of Partick Thistle, Aston Villa and Scotland with his unsurpassed defensive qualities, stylish and artistic play, as well as uncanny positional sense.

The sturdy Scot played nine times for his country and proved himself to be a fine Villa captain in the immediate post-war period. George's achievements on the football field were many, but perhaps, he will best be remembered as the only full-back to regularly make the wonderful Stanley Matthews appear like an average player. Yes, this marvellous footballer's defensive strengths made great wingers ordinary and his constructive play helped make ordinary wingers great!

Cummings' habit of thwarting the ambitions of the most formidable of opponents is legendary. But, how did the highly mobile lump of wrought iron which was George Cummings in his heyday manage to contain the awesome adversary that was Stanley Matthews?

A Norman Edwards cartoon paying tribute to Stanley Matthews on the occasion of his fiftieth birthday—1 February 1965.

"I just didn't give him space, son," the great full-back once told me. "You daren't rush in on Stan or he would make an utter fool of you. I approached him in a crab-like fashion, forcing him out to the touchline, but always making sure that he didn't manage to get one of those dangerous crosses over. You had to keep your eyes firmly fixed on the ball and not allow yourself to be distracted by his body movements . . . . every player, even the very best, has a 'bogey man', and I just happened to be Stan's," said George, adding; "I first played against Matthews in the 1930s, during his first spell with Stoke City. Quite early in the game we came face to face, with Stan in possession. He brought the ball up to me, stopped and then began that little jig which was to mesmerise so many full-backs. I watched these antics for a while and then said to myself, 'If I'm going to stand here dancing with you, I'm never going to get the ball.' So I went in and got it."

"Oh, Stan was a great player . . . but I never used to lose any sleep over playing him the next day," George once said. "I think I can say in all honesty that Matthews never had a good game at Villa Park while I was around . . . he never made a monkey out of me!"

"During his days with Stoke City and Blackpool, Stan and I faced up to each other many times and I must have got the better of him in at least ninety per cent of those games," claimed George. "Not long before I retired, in 1949, we played Blackpool at home and I said to Stan that he must feel relieved that I was finally about to hang up my boots, because that would mean he could have a good game at Villa Park . . . Stan just smiled and said, 'Yes I will, but it's about time because you are getting on a bit, George.' I think he appreciated that one," added Cummings. "Perhaps Stan was sad himself that our friendly rivalry, which had added many thousands to the gates, was coming to an end."

Intrigued, I simply had to get Sir Stanley's thoughts on his clashes with the Villa defender. Always a gentleman, I was confident that the man who was knighted in recognition of his tremendous contribution to the sport would respond to the letter which I sent to the Matthews' home in Canada. Respond he did, saying:

George was in the tradition of so many fine Scottish full-backs. He was big, immensely strong, tough, hard, quite fearless and, for his size, extremely agile. When he came in to tackle you knew all about it, because he timed those tackles to absolute perfection. George Cummings was one of the finest full-backs of all time, as I know only too well. The Villa man and I had many tussles and, in all honesty, I was never too happy or successful when playing against him.

What a fine tribute from a man who is rightly acknowledged and revered as being one of the greatest soccer players of all time.

Partick Thistle manager, Donald Turner, was quick to realise that he had made a very special capture after managing to sign eighteen-year-old George Cummings from Grange Rovers on 6 June 1932. In fact, the astute Turner outfoxed many interested clubs and secured the lad's signature in the nick of time, because he arrived in the Cummings household just half an hour before the young player was due to head for Glasgow and a rendezvous with Celtic manager, Willie Maley, in that city's Bank Restaurant. As it was, Turner was able to persuade George to join Partick Thistle . . . and so the lad missed that Glasgow-bound train and failed to keep his appointment with Mr Maley when it had seemed odds-on that he was destined to become a Celt.

That contract which George signed guaranteed him a weekly pay packet of £3 in the close season, £4 during the season and built-in bonuses of £2 for a win and £1 for a draw . . . provided he was playing in the first team! Having agreed those terms with Cummings and secured his prize capture, Turner switched the defender from right to left-back when Firhill favourite, Jimmy Rae, was transferred to Plymouth Argyle. So the craggy full-back, whose

Partick Thistle FC, Glasgow and Charity Cup winners, 1934–35. Back row left to right: W. Miller, A. Elliot, R. Donnelly, G. Cummings, R. Johnstone, E. McLeod, H. Baigrie, G. Wylie. Front row left to right: D. Turner (Secretary/Manager), A. McSpadyen, J. Wyllie, P. Bain, S. Calderwood, A. Hastie, R. Regan, J. Kennedy (Trainer).

pawky sense of humour brought many a chuckle from his team-mates and was reflected in his play, embarked on what was to prove an illustrious career.

Partick Thistle's Firhill ground is situated in the Queen's Cross area of Glasgow and in the early 1930s it was a busy, highly populated environment with countless tramcars threading their way through the bustling life of the grimy tenements. Illuminated nightly by the lamplighter, those gas-lit streets reflected a high degree of poverty in the days before the so-called cushion of the Welfare State. It was in those very streets that a little lad called Bobby Campbell happily spent much of his time. Bobby was an avid "Jags" fan and the bedroom walls in that Benview Street home of his were lovingly decorated with pictures of his Thistle heroes . . . Miller, Donnelly, Johnstone, but, most importantly of all, George Cummings.

Cummings was the little lad's idol, and almost every day the twelve-year-old would take the long road back from North Kelvinside School, hoping to catch a glimpse of his hero. You can imagine young Bobby's delight when his pal, who was the son of Partick Thistle trainer, Jim Kennedy, told him that the track around the Firhill pitch had been widened to accommodate dog racing and that the coveted and responsible post of ball boy was "up for grabs" if Bobby wanted to team up with him and accept the challenge. Needless to say he didn't have to be asked twice. So little Campbell donned the black and white rig-out of a Firhill ball boy and happily shared centre stage with his heroes.

George Cummings, the superstar and Bobby Campbell, the diminutive, adoring ball boy became the best of friends and, before each and every home match, the classy defender would give his new-found pal pieces of chewing-gum. Now in his sixties and living in Bristol, Campbell recalls those days with tremendous affection. "I thought I was in heaven," he says. "It was hard to believe, but there I was, changing in the ball and boot room next to the Thistle dressing-room, mingling with my favourites and being given chewing gum by the man whose face was all over my bedroom walls."

Bobby was heartbroken when George joined Aston Villa in November 1935. "I remember crying my eyes out," he says. That unhappy youngster could never have dreamt that in days to come his path and the path of the great George Cummings were to cross again.

It was hardly surprising that George became such a great player, because football was the blood which flowed in the very veins of the male members of the Cummings family. His father had played in goal for Stockport County, while George was only one of four footballing brothers to join Aston Villa. His arrival in the Midlands in 1935 was the signal for full-backs Fred and David, along with goalkeeper, Bill, to follow him to the club. But only George remained at Villa Park.

Shortly after joining Aston Villa the talented defender completed the highly prized honour of a "triple cap", after playing against Ireland, Wales and England in the same season. But 1935–36 was a disastrous season for Villa because George Cummings, the established international player, found himself, with many other similarly recognised stars, relegated to the Second Division. However, by season 1937–38 the Midlands club were back in the top sphere where they belonged, thanks mainly to the tremendous defensive formation which had been established. "We met Preston in the FA Cup semi-final that season," Cummings once said, growling with more than a hint of anger in his voice. "Although we scored first, they beat us 2–1. We were the only team to score against them in the Cup and they went on to win it . . . they beat us with a goal that was at least twenty yards offside!"

George loved to relate the tale of an occasion when Aston Villa almost sparked off an international incident while touring Germany in 1938:

> England faced the Germans in the Berlin stadium which staged the 1938 Olympics. It was 14 May and we were due to play a German/Austrian select at the same venue on the following day . . . so the Villa lads were all at the match. The English team respectfully gave the Nazi salute when the German anthem was played. But, when it came to *God Save the King*, the Germans kept their arms in the air and showed no respect whatsoever. Alex Massie, a Scottish international team-mate and I watched, steam coming out of our ears and making up our minds, there and then, that Villa would be giving no Nazi salute when we played next day.

Berlin 1938 . . . and the England team (white shirts) give the Nazi salute.

Determined in their resolve to snub those cocky Germans when their turn came, those Scottish international stars sat back and happily watched the English lads beat their arrogant hosts by six goals to three.

It must have been over eighty degrees in the shade when we lined up in front of a huge German crowd, which included Dr Josef Goebbels and many other high-ranking Nazi officials. Before the kick-off, while the home side were giving that damn salute, we practised shooting in at goal as we would do at home, keeping those arms firmly by our sides. The crowd whistled and booed us, but still we wouldn't give the salute. The Germans had placed buckets of iced water around the track so that their players could nip off and refresh themselves during the match. When the play was at the other end of the park I went over expecting to be allowed a drink from one of the buckets, but a German steward rushed over and tried to chase me away. To say that I was mad would be an understatement. Seething with rage, I booted the bucket into the air and a none-too-chuffed German crowd roared for my blood. At the end of the game, which we won 3–2, the select side gave the Nazi salute again, while we just strolled off the field with the jeers of the crowd ringing in our ears.

Those incidents caused a terrible rumpus and Aston Villa were slated in the German press to such an extent that the club chairman called the players together, told them that he was extremely concerned at the scale of the adverse reaction and said that the tour could be cut short. The Villa players certainly didn't want that to happen and reluctantly agreed to give the Nazi salute at their last match . . . but they had made their point!

When, in September 1939, the mindless and evil doctrine of insanity that is Fascism, coupled with Adolf Hitler's fanatical obsession to create a master race, plunged Europe into an inevitable and fearsome war, George Cummings "signed on" at the Labour Exchange fully expecting to be drafted into the forces. But George's skills as a metal worker were needed at home and he was transferred to Dunlop's to help the war effort by preparing Rolls-Royce Merlin aircraft engines. Cummings guested with Birmingham, Nottingham Forest and Northampton Town, before heading back to Scotland to marry his girlfriend, Beth, on St Valentine's Day 1941. While he was north of the border, Falkirk Football Club gratefully seized the opportunity to avail themselves of his services and George played a few matches for the Brockville club before returning to where his heart was firmly anchored . . . Villa Park.

Surprisingly, even as a lad living in Scotland, George had been a keen Villa fan and his great affection for the club could be traced back to his early schooldays. "I loved Villa," he once said. "When I pulled on a claret and blue jersey I used to say to myself: 'They will score over my dead body'."

Like many players of his generation the war robbed Cummings of many more full international caps and, probably, major honours at club level. But, when the hostilities were over, the old war horse continued to assume his role in the left-back berth of the Villa defence, taking over the captaincy from Alex Massie when the stylish Scottish wing-half was elevated to the position of club manager.

Remember that little ball boy, Bobby Campbell? What had become of him? Well, while George Cummings was carving out a top-class reputation for himself on the English side of the border, Bobby was developing into a fine footballer in his own right. The slim, dark-haired forward played for Scottish Junior side, Glasgow Perthshire, and signed for Falkirk Football Club in August 1941. Following five years in the services, during which time he continued to play for the ''Bairns'' for a spell before being posted overseas, Bobby was transferred to Chelsea in May 1947. Although Campbell's versatility meant he could be fielded in any forward position, outside-right was where he enjoyed playing most and where Bobby became established as a first-rate goal-maker and no slouch himself when it came to hitting the back of the net.

Chelsea had paid Falkirk £8,900 for Campbell's signature but his Stamford Bridge debut was delayed because, before he could kick a ball for the club, Bobby fell ill and the club doctor insisted that he should return to Scotland and rest for at least a month. When Chelsea manager, Billy Birrell, informed Campbell of the doctor's decision, Bobby begged to have the period of convalescence reduced, so desperate was he to establish himself in the Londoners' first team. Birrell fully appreciated Bobby's disappointment but explained that he had no alternative other than to accept the medical advice. You can imagine the manager's astonishment when Campbell insisted that his wages be cut during his absence because he felt he had let the club down.

Perhaps, though, the wingman's enforced lay-off was pre-ordained, because when he finally lined up in that Chelsea number seven jersey on the first Saturday in October 1947, the ''Pensioners'' opponents were none other than Aston Villa! Unbelievably, there in that Villa number three shirt was the familiar and distinguished figure of the bald-headed veteran of many a campaign . . . George Cummings!

''I approached George just before the kick-off and asked if he recognised me,'' says Bobby laughing and adding, ''He looked me up and down before responding gruffly, 'No, I've never seen you before, son.' I then told George that I was wee Bobby Campbell from Firhill, the little ball boy to whom he had given chewing-gum all those years ago.'' With a face mirroring his total bewilderment and to the utter astonishment of the crowd, Cummings hugged

Bobby Campbell . . . Chelsea and Scotland.

Bobby, saying, "What are you doing here? Bloody hell, son, don't make me feel any older than I am." Yes, the paths of the ball boy and his hero had crossed again! They were reunited in remarkable circumstances and the most unexpected of settings. "It was a great moment, but suddenly George's attitude changed," recalls the ex-Stamford Bridge star. "Realising that we were in direct opposition to each other he leaned across and said, 'Listen, son, don't take it personally . . . but I'm going to have to give you a hard time.'"

For Campbell the fairytale was far from over. After a great joust with the man who was still his hero, Chelsea won 4–2 and Bobby scored the first two goals for the Stamford Bridge side. At the end of what was a dream debut for the former ball boy from Benview Street, George patted him on the head, saying, "Well done, Bobby lad. You had a fine game." And, as far as Campbell was concerned, *that* was the ultimate compliment!

Bobby Campbell scores on his Chelsea debut, watched by George Cummings.

The great Tommy Walker, Heart of Midlothian, Chelsea and Scotland.

The right-winger was the new-found hero of Stamford Bridge and while the great Tommy Lawton, who had scored the other Chelsea goals, left the ground in comparative anonymity, the debutant was besieged by autograph hunters. "That great gentleman of football, Tommy Walker, told me the kids should never leave disappointed and that, however long it takes, they should get their signature," says Bobby. So Campbell asked the young fans to line up in an organised queue which stretched for over fifty yards and, twenty minutes later, every book and scrap of paper was signed and everyone went home happy, including, I suspect, the man who hated to lose . . . George Cummings!

Campbell's fine play quickly caught the eye of the Scottish selectors and he was capped five times for his country. The winger also played for Reading and, among other positions held in football, managed Dumbarton and Bristol Rovers. After a lifetime in the game, Bobby Campbell still regards George Cummings as the greatest defender he ever set eyes on. "George was, without doubt, the 'daddy of them all'," he says. "His left peg was brilliant and every ball was measured to perfection . . . and I'm not just saying that because George was my hero and so generous to me when I was a kid," concludes Bobby with a smile.

BBC radio football reporter and journalist, Larry Canning, a post-war team-mate of Cummings, has very fond memories of his former captain. "Wherever George stood the ball landed at his feet," says Larry. "But it was no coincidence because he had a positional sense which could not be taught and that, more than anything else, made the man different. He was an astute tactician who could get opponents running yards in the wrong direction without him even touching the ball. From the time I arrived at Villa Park when I was sixteen, I always regarded the great man as a big brother figure," adds Canning. "I played my first game after the war in 1948. It was at Highbury against Arsenal. We lost, and afterwards a well known journalist came into our dressing-room to ask me how I thought I had played. I told him he should ask our captain. 'How do you think he played, George?' the reporter enquired. Our skipper, relaxing in the communal bath while puffing his cigarette, thought for a moment then declared: 'Considering he played the Arsenal, the referee and the two linesmen, I thought he had a ******* blinder!'"

Too many stars to mention refer to Cummings as the finest full-back of them all. But who did the hero of Villa Park rate as his most difficult opponent? "It would have to be Tom Finney," he once told me. "Tom was two-footed and a real bundle of tricks. But if you were to ask me who was the best player I ever saw, it would definitely be George Best . . . because George had everything," said Cummings. "On his day the Irishman was virtually unstoppable . . . he may even have presented me with a few problems!"

Two of the very best . . . Georgie Best (right) pictured at Old Trafford with the great Denis Law.

Naturally, George's widow, Beth, a real gem of a person, knew the great full-back better than anyone. ''My George had a great passion for the game,'' she says. ''He would arrive home after playing a match battered, bruised and with deep ruts on his bald head through heading the lace on that heavy old ball. The great players of George's day never received the rewards which they should have done. Having played a game at Villa Park he would come out of the ground with his pal and team-mate, Freddie Haycock. They would walk between the rows of posh cars, which belonged to the directors and their friends, put on bicycle clips and ride off on a couple of old bikes . . . both of which happened to belong to Freddie!'' says Beth with a smile and a shrug of the shoulders. ''When you really think about it, it was a disgrace! How shameful . . . those stars who were pulling in the crowds and making the club rich, pedalling home on a couple of old bikes! Men like George were exploited . . . there is no other word for it! But football brought tremendous pleasure to his life and gave him years of happiness. That's more important than anything, isn't it?''

In common with so many truly great players, George's weaknesses were his strengths, his strengths his weaknesses. He played football in the belief that his playing days would never end, that those sturdy legs of his could keep pounding across the turf forever. I have always felt that the more famous the player, the harder it is for him to adapt to the personal trauma that is retirement. Understandably, the once great star, perhaps acting in a back-room capacity, finds it difficult to take instructions from a manager who has never even remotely matched his status as a player. George was unlucky, because those war years cost him many honours and, had he only been born a few years later, his talents would, no doubt, have guaranteed his future in financial terms. As it was he had to earn a living working in factories. But George Cummings was not the kind of man to expect or invite favours from anyone.

It makes me absolutely sick when I see second-rate golfers, who have hardly won a major tournament in their lives, becoming millionaires! And even more angry when I realise how much the snooker stars earn in this day and age. Apart from the vast fortunes which those snooker players make touring the professional circuit, they collect more cash from one year's sponsorship and advertising deals than truly great sportsmen such as George Cummings earned from nearly two decades of dedicated service to football!

We Britons talk a lot and are very adept at ''blowing our own trumpets''. But, in reality, we don't give a damn when it comes to the great sporting stars of the past. Our tendency is to think only of the present, to look inwardly, while perceiving life through rose-tinted spectacles . . . and we have very short memories! How many times have you heard some football chairman referring

George (left) with ex-team-mate, Freddie Haycock,
at Villa's centenary celebrations in 1974.

to his club as a ''family club''? Their concept of the size of that family falls far short of mine. Wouldn't it be nice if those clubs took the time to do a simple thing like send a Xmas card to the men who served them so well . . . it can mean so much, so very much! I am not, I hasten to add, referring to any organisation in particular, but pointing an accusing finger at almost every club in the land. In my opinion we have a long, long way to go before we can truly call ourselves a football-loving nation.

Wilf Mannion, that fine Middlesbrough and England inside-forward, once said this to me: ''Jim, you think you know a lot about football. But only those who have played the game at the highest level really know what it's all about. Only they know how it feels to face the frightening reality that those playing days are over. You spend years being idolised by huge crowds, knowing that you can confidently match your skills against those of any player in the world. Then, suddenly, it's all behind you. At an early age you are forced to accept the fact that you will never re-create or soak up such comparable glories again . . . and you look ahead towards an uncertain future, because soccer is all that you know!''

George Cummings shared my opinion that George Best was the greatest footballer of them all. In his autobiography, *Where Do I Go From Here*, Best makes an interesting and relevant point, based on his experiences in the USA:

> Whereas in Britain the sporting hero is of value only while he's at the top of his career, in America he can cash in on his name and fame for many years afterwards. For example: I'd switch on the television and there, in a commercial, might be Jesse Owens, or a footballer or baseball star from twenty or thirty years back. The man still meant something to the people. How many sporting heroes of the past are seen on British television? Henry Cooper maybe, but that's because he made himself a personality in his own right. What does Bobby Moore advertise on television these days, or Terry Downes? In America their equivalents would be recognised and respected for their achievements long after they've retired. But in Britain, so it seems, no one wants to know you once you've had your day.

George Cummings hailed from the industrial central belt of Scotland, an area which, per head of population, has probably produced more truly great footballers than any other part of the United Kingdom. He was one of that very special breed of men who had the mantle of stardom thrust upon them from an early age, one of a select few who can accurately be counted among the all-time greats of football. But George was more than just a first-rate player. From all accounts, he was a distinctive personality and top-class entertainer, one whose immense talent and charismatic personality had the power and rare quality of attracting huge heaps of shillings to the turnstiles.

A last word on the late, great Partick Thistle, Aston Villa and Scotland defender goes to his former team-mate, Larry Canning, who, as a player and broadcaster, has been involved in football for well over forty years. ''George Cummings was, undoubtedly, the greatest of them all,'' says Larry. ''I will remember him with enormous affection and gratitude for giving me the immense pleasure of witnessing at close quarters how our lovely game should be played . . . and so will many thousands of others.''

10

THE MAN FOR ALL SEASONS

When asked to name the best defenders he had "crossed swords with" during the course of an illustrious career, the peerless Tom Finney, that English firebrand whose skill and blistering pace scorched the hair off the knees of many a world-class full-back during his Preston North End and England days, smiled and replied: "You may be surprised to hear me say this, but they were both Scots. The best players I played against were George Cummings and George Young, according to whether I was playing on the right wing or the left." Finney went on, "Cummings simply ignored me. I could waggle my body, throw out my hands . . . it made no difference . . . George kept his eyes firmly glued on the ball. He paid little or no attention to how I moved . . . but when the ball moved . . . ah, that was different!"

And what about George Young? Finney sighed, "Young simply led you up the garden path," he said. "You'd swing a hip and run past him. Then, just as you were about to cross the ball, a long limb reached past you and you were left swiping at the air. There were many occasions when I refused to believe that Big George had only two legs . . . he was like a giant octopus which sucked you into its tentacles."

There must be something in the air circulating around a certain Stirlingshire town which breathes life into great defenders . . . because both Georges hailed from the Grangemouth area, both played for the local Grange Rovers, both men became great captains and on-field tacticians and both men will go down in soccer history counted among the finest defensive players ever known to the game!

Character. In every sense that's the word which best describes George Lewis Young, former skipper of Glasgow Rangers and Scotland. Capped fifty-three times at full international level between 1946 and 1957, the six foot two inch giant captained his country on no fewer than forty-eight occasions. George played twenty-one times for the Scottish League and, in 1955, was voted "Scottish Footballer of the Year". At club level "Mr Big" won six

George Young, captain of Glasgow Rangers and Scotland.

League Championship medals, four Scottish Cup winner's badges and two League Cup winner's medals, in almost 700 first team matches for his only senior club . . . the famous Glasgow Rangers!

Born in Grangemouth in 1922, George Young was destined to become one of football's most illustrious captains. The son of a railwayman, he was a Scottish Schoolboy international star in the 1930s and played in Falkirk and District representative sides alongside such lads as goalkeeper, Bobby Brown, later to become his Rangers and Scotland team-mate as well as international team manager, Eddie Turnbull, a member of Hibernian's "Famous Five" forward line, Davie Lapsley, St Mirren's inspirational captain when the Love Street side won the Scottish Cup for the second time in 1959 and last, but certainly not least, the great Billy Steel! Big George and wee Billy, who were also Scottish Schoolboy international team-mates, were known as Mutt and Jeff in those days and they went on to become two of Scotland's most famous footballing sons. Between 1947 and 1953, while starring for Greenock Morton, Derby County and Dundee, the pocket-sized dynamo that was Billy Steel

No it's not a scene from Bugsy Malone . . . *but a group of Scottish Schoolboy internationalists in the 1930s. Would you have recognised George Young (centre) and Billy Steel (second from left at front)?*

played thirty times for his country. A flash of Steel was sufficient to instil fear and trepidation into the hearts of the finest defenders, because the quicksilver and lethal goal-grabber was one of the game's greatest ever inside-forwards.

Billy's schoolboy chum, George Young, who earned undying fame for his defensive qualities, was nicknamed "Corky" during his senior playing career, due to the fact that he became the owner of one of football's most famous lucky charms! After Rangers had beaten Morton in the 1948 Scottish Cup Final, recording their first post-war victory in the competition, the trophy was filled with champagne at the club's celebration dinner. To his surprise a waiter handed George the cork from the first bottle of "bubbly" which was popped, saying: "Keep this . . . it will bring you luck." George did indeed keep the cork and Dame Fortune smiled on him. In October 1948 Scotland were fortunate enough to defeat Wales in Cardiff and, a month later, Ireland were beaten 3–2 at Hampden. Then, on Saturday, 9 April 1949, came the crucial clash with England at Wembley. George dropped the good luck charm into a blazer pocket before travelling to London. Scotland won 3–1, with his old schoolboy pal, Billy Steel, grabbing one of the goals, and the Scots were crowned British Champions. So that tiny cork and its giant owner became overnight legends!

George Young—monarch of all he surveyed.

The monarch of all he surveyed in a fantastic senior playing career which spanned sixteen years, George Young strode across the Scottish game like a Colossus, winning the admiration of friend and foe alike. A magnificent defender at right-back or centre-half, a born leader and a great tactician, George was always scrupulously fair. Amazingly, during his reign as undisputed "King" of Scottish football, the big fella' was booked only *once* and *never* sent off. Although Young recalls where he was cautioned, he just can't remember when and against whom. "I felt very ashamed and, maybe, that's why I pushed the incident to the back of my mind," says George. "I know that it happened at Hampden and that Jack Mowatt was the referee. Jack took my name for talking out of turn when I should have known better and kept my big mouth shut."

The modern players who have led Rangers in recent seasons and who have, on occasions, been favourably compared with the "Gentle Giant", can't even begin to match that kind of disciplinary record, can they? And they certainly won't be playing football at Ibrox for . . . sixteen years!

Young cost Rangers the princely sum of £75 when he joined that club from the eloquently named Kirkintilloch Rob Roy in September 1941. In fact the Rangers defence in which George played and which became collectively known as "The Iron Curtain", joined those "Light Blues" for little more than a few pounds. Bobby Brown, George Young, Jock "Tiger" Shaw, Ian McColl, Willie Woodburn and Sammy Cox . . . those great defenders all played for Scotland and amassed 122 full caps between them. Who would have thought that one day the heroes of the Ibrox rear-guard would be English and not Scottish internationalists!

"Old Bill" Struth.

Young's great mentor, Bill Struth, adored his captain and once the Rangers side was chosen "Old Bill", as George affectionately calls that greatest of Ibrox managers, simply took his seat in the stand, secure in the knowledge that the "Light Blues" fortunes were in the most capable and caring of hands. Likewise, Sir George Graham, Secretary of the Scottish Football Association, was content to let "Corky" get on with the business at hand after the International Selection Committee had chosen the Scottish side. Indeed, Young's stature was such that, on occasions, he not only captained the Scottish team but also named the eleven men who would represent their country.

George Young was a proud Ranger, cast in the mould and traditions of one of the world's greatest football clubs, and his commitment to the joint cause of Glasgow Rangers and Scotland was total. "I had a leg in plaster on six occasions, my nose was broken several times and a bad achilles tendon injury kept me out for months," says George, adding, "Over the seasons those big bones of mine took many a hard knock."

Scotland versus England 1956 . . . and George Young introduces the Duke of Gloucester to Airdrie's Ian MacMillan.

Big "Corky" hung up his boots in 1957 and was not directly involved with football until becoming Third Lanark's manager in 1959. With his unbeatable eye for spotting a promising player and the ability to blend varied talents into an effective and attractive unit, he built a fine side on a shoestring budget while at Cathkin. Young had all the credentials and if destiny had only ordained that he become Scotland's team manager, many believe that George would have put Scottish international football into the game's very top drawer. Today, when George Young tells me that a player is "promising", I take careful note because, virtually without fail, that assessment turns out to be 100 per cent accurate. What a tragedy it is that his vast experience is not utilised in some capacity today.

But George is a giant of a man in every way. Aside from his fantastic record on the football field, he has worked endlessly and tirelessly on behalf of many different charities and, since his playing days, has been particularly closely involved with the Erskine Hospital for Ex-Servicemen's Paraplegic Coach and Comforts Fund, personally raising large sums of money to ensure that those ex-servicemen enjoy some of the comforts which they so richly deserve. George inherited this involvement from Bill Struth, and his commitment has lasted for well over thirty years, largely unsung at his own insistence. Sports writer, Allan Herron, summed up Scotland's greatest ever captain to absolute perfection when he described "Corky" as "a gentle man, who did too many favours for too many people".

But "Mr Big" derives more pleasure from giving than from receiving. I recall being in his company on an outing which he had organised for some of his friends from Erskine Hospital to a Clyde versus Morton match at Shawfield. George helped to get his pals out of the coach and to see them safely into the ground in their wheelchairs. After a lot of coming and going mixed with good-humoured banter, the lads were positioned in those chairs and ready to enjoy the match. Thinking that they looked like the Shawfield greyhounds lined up in their traps before a race, the big man raised the heartiest laugh of the day when he said loudly and jokingly, "I don't know about you, Jim . . . but my money's on Willie in trap four."

The following little tale also typifies the man. In the late 1950s a lad called Jim Crawford broke an arm shortly before he was due to play for the Scottish Schoolboys in a representative match. On hearing of the boy's misfortune George tracked down his parents and invited the whole family to a consolation slap-up meal in the Clyde Valley's Tillietudlem Hotel, which the ex-Rangers and Scotland skipper then owned. Almost thirty years later, Jim Crawford, who hadn't met the former Ibrox idol before or since, was seated at a film show arranged in "Corky's" honour when, to his utter astonishment, George approached him and said: "Nice to see you, Jim. How's the arm?" Yes, that's George Young!

Now a well respected Glasgow entrepreneur and businessman, former Ibrox ball boy, Jim McCosh, also has fond memories of Geordie Young. "All of the Rangers players were great to the ball boys . . . but George was a bit special," says Jim. "Remember when modern, lightweight boots first came into vogue in the 1950s? Geordie Niven, the Rangers 'keeper, was finding difficulty in getting distance with his goal kicks when wearing them and I was thrilled when George Young threw the very expensive boots to me, saying, "Take these, Jim lad. Niven canny kick with them.""

Young Jim's family home was situated in Copland Road, within the shadow of Ibrox Stadium, and he remembers a time when his brother, Hunter McCosh, had broken a leg playing football in the Ibrox car park. "George heard that my brother's leg was in plaster and that he was unable to get to the matches," says Jim, adding, "Big George would arrive at our home before the match, lift Hunter on to his shoulders and carry him down the stairs from our tenement home to a waiting car. On arriving at the stadium, he would carry Hunter to a seat in the stand and, after playing in the match, take my delighted brother home again, lifting him up those three flights of stairs. How can we possibly forget George Young?"

I challenge anyone to name a footballer who has devoted as much time to helping others as has George Young! Believe me, many would be astounded and greatly enlightened if made fully aware of the extent to which Geordie has shown willingness to lend a helping hand when it was most needed.

The praise and respect which this great humanitarian earned during his playing career was virtually universal. Tom Finney is, by no means, the only top English forward of the time to describe George Young's defensive qualities in glowing terms. Wilf Mannion, that marvellous Middlesbrough and England inside-forward, known as "The Golden Boy of Soccer", shares Finney's high opinion of Young. "George was one of the greatest defenders I ever played against," says Wilf. "The big man was a truly wonderful sportsman . . . but he gave absolutely nothing away." The "Maestro" himself, touchline terror, Stanley Matthews, also had a very high opinion of George Young's football talents. "George had long legs and they were hard to pass.

Wilf Mannion . . . "Big George was a marvellous sportsman".

But he was always one of the great Scots and when I saw him in a line-up I knew winning wouldn't be easy.'' Yet another member of the "Auld Enemy", centre-forward, Jackie Milburn of Newcastle United, also put George into the game's top bracket. "He was one of the best centre-halves I've ever seen,'' said the late, great Milburn. "I wish he was still playing, just to show what

Jackie Milburn, Newcastle United and England.

men like me were up against. One thing, he was extremely hard without being dirty. Another was his talking during a match. If he knocked you down, he would pick you up, pat you on the head and say, 'Never mind, son, try again.' He would even congratulate you if you beat him.'' And finally, that jocular and much-loved Irishman, the incomparable Charlie Tully, who played for Rangers' arch-rivals, Glasgow Celtic, summed up how difficult it was to pass the defensive wall that was George Young. "You could run at that big fella with the ball at your feet, beat him four or five times in the one move and, somehow, still not manage to pass him.''

*Two of Young's great rivals . . . Celtic's Charlie Tully (left)
and John "Hooky" McPhail.*

When George Young's long-time friend, Don Revie, heard that the "Gentle Giant" had never received a benefit or been honoured with a testimonial match he was "flabbergasted". With admirable enthusiasm Don approached Rangers, asking them to make their ground available and to co-operate with him in organising a benefit match for their former captain. Rangers declined, stating that by honouring Young they would be setting a precedent. But Don Revie was as resolute and determined as an English bulldog and the character-istics which helped to make him such a fine player and manager made him all the more determined to succeed. I felt deeply honoured when asked to join the committee which Don formed on George Young's behalf. I was, and always will be, totally convinced of the fact that it was a great and just cause. After all, hadn't Tom Finney, Denis Law, Stanley Matthews, Gordon Smith, George Best, Billy Liddell, Bobby Charlton, Billy Bremner, John Greig, and many others all had testimonial matches? I firmly believe that George Young, who is of equal standing to those all-time greats and who has done as much for football as any other player in the history of the game, was fully deserving of such a tribute. Besides, unlike many of those famous names, Young had been "aye ready" and willing to devote his entire senior career in giving unstinting loyalty to just one club!

That testimonial committee worked wholeheartedly on George Young's behalf and, at the end of the day and all things considered, we were relatively successful. Many good folks helped our cause, including ex-Rangers and Scotland stars, Willie Woodburn, Alex Scott, Sammy Cox, Bobby Shearer, Jim Baxter and Colin Jackson as well as former Celtic internationalists, Sean Fallon, John McPhail and Jim Brogan. Graeme Souness, then with Italian club, Sampdoria, was kind enough to send over one of his jerseys for auction . . . a gesture which was gratefully received.

George Young's testimonial match between English and Scottish select sides was played at Falkirk's ground on 11 May 1986 and sadly, although Rangers did supply players, despite frequent requests they failed to send their big-name and potentially crowd-pulling stars to Brockville. The testimonial dinner, held in a Glasgow hotel, was a glittering occasion but, although they had booked a table for ten, the hierarchy of the Ibrox boardroom failed to show face and that candlelit table was conspicuously empty.

We are, as "Bauldie" of *The Scottish Referee* had pointed out in 1905 when reflecting on the achievements of the Old Vale, only on this "old solid 'ba" called Earth for a very short time. Comparatively speaking, for not all that much longer than it takes one of those candles to burn out and die . . . and our fragile lives can be extinguished with a single puff and without warning. The fact that Rangers snubbed their most capped player, thereby missing the opportunity of a short lifetime to honour a true and faithful servant as well as to demonstrate a little kindness and understanding, is sad, very sad. Big Geordie simply didn't deserve to be treated in such a scandalous fashion. There is absolutely no doubting what that other truly great Glasgow Ranger, Bill Struth, would have had to say about the manner in which his much-loved and trusted skipper was treated.

Despite the hurtful treatment which "Corky" received, the fact is that he played a huge part in the tale of the long trail of glory that is the story of Glasgow Rangers Football Club. Yes, the man has contributed much, much more to sport than those often faceless and insensitive pontificators who are found in the boardrooms of most clubs and football associations and who, alas, play a part in controlling the destiny of our great game. Waxing eloquent, the majority of those sporting autocrats couldn't even begin to hold a candle to the likes of George Young. Doubtless he gets on their wick because they cannot even begin to comprehend the man or to identify qualities such as loyalty, integrity and kindness, for which big George is famous.

These boardroom barristers forget that they are merely football caretakers and that the game simply doesn't belong to them. Those fortunate enough to possess the capital can treat themselves to a Rolls-Royce car or a villa in Spain but, in reality, nobody, but nobody, can purchase a football club! Soccer is like no other business, because clubs such as Rangers, Celtic, Manchester City and West Ham, for instance, belong to the armies of devoted fans whose families have nurtured the traditions of that favourite team for generations. In essence, football also belongs to those great players who made the game, many of whom were exploited and robbed of their just rewards. They may not have piles of shares tucked away in a bank vault, but no one is going to tell me that the players and fans are not co-owners of the game of football.

It has to be admitted, though, that there are still fine legislators and men of vision involved in our beloved sport. However, such individuals are somewhat thin on the ground, almost as hard to find as a photograph of Celtic's Paul McStay in the Rangers souvenir shop, or a Torquay United supporters' club in Aberdeen. Life is indeed short, just like a flickering candle, and we can't take power and wealth with us into the next world, can we? But when the last great soccer historian comes to put pen to paper and produce the definitive work on the story of football, he will devote an entire chapter, not to those money-mad moguls of the boardroom, but to a big laddie from Grangemouth who ignited many of Scottish football's candles and who, on and off the football field, lit up many a life.

The attitude displayed by the men controlling Rangers in 1986 is, it has to be said, in no way untypical. Although there are a few notable exceptions, most clubs treat their former stars in a manner akin to a little boy who throws some old, disused toy into a dark corner of the loft and forgets about it until, perhaps many years later, he stumbles across it and is momentarily filled with nostalgia. You won't hear George Young complaining but today he suffers from crippling arthritis, a lasting and extremely painful reminder of those many injuries and of years of commitment on the football field. Unlike film stars or recording artists who earn vast fortunes and receive royalties from their work for the rest of their lives, the vast majority of the stars of the world's most popular entertainment, in the long term, get precious little reward for their efforts. Having gained first-hand experience of the attitude of most clubs to the heroes of the past, I don't blame the modern player for ''making hay while the sun shines'' and grabbing all that he can from what is a short and risky career. Believe me, fifty years from now, when you're hirpling along Oxford Street in London or hobbling down Edinburgh's Royal Mile, remembering international appearances and longingly recalling those playing days, the chances are that the ''grand old club'' which you served so well won't even be aware that, although you're not kicking any more, you are still very much alive! By then the lavishly refurbished boardroom will be populated by the next generation of family dynasties which control many of the clubs or predominantly egotistical businessmen who have managed to purchase a seat on some board of directors . . . none of whom will be aware of the huge contribution which you made because your name just won't ring any bells! And, if we don't get back to the days when footballers enjoyed much more freedom for self-expression, by then coaches will predetermine the results of football matches on computers with the help of mathematicians, while the players are reduced to little more than robots!

Why is it that life so often appears to be a conspiracy of the selfish against the unselfish, of the unimaginative against the imaginative, and of the uncaring against the caring?

In common with every human being, big George Young has his faults and there are those who do not share my great affection for the man. Young's friends are well aware of the fact that George has fallen foul of narrow-minded people because he has never been afraid to voice an opinion, however controversial. Not a man to "sit on the fence", at no time has "Corky" paid lip service or grovelled to anyone, whatever their status. Ironically these are the very qualities which, when allied to his considerable talents as a footballer, endeared the man to a nation and earned him the reputation of being one of sport's finest ever ambassadors!

For six months of my life I was honoured to be a member of The George Young Testimonial Committee. During those days I got to know George very well as we toured the clubs together with a video road show. On one occasion we shared a room in Aberdeen's Imperial Hotel and, for me, it was a real eye-opening experience. Our room was tucked away in the bowels of the building, at the end of a seemingly endless maze of corridors and stairways. Away from the public glare it quickly became evident to me that the big man's legs were causing him terrible pain. I walked down those long passages with the twenty-one-stone frame of George Young leaning heavily on my straining shoulders, before we finally reached our room and the big fellow was able to rest on his bed. George will be furious with me for including that incident within these pages . . . but I cannot emphasise enough the injustices which George Young and many other legends of the game have suffered.

The motive behind the non-appearance of any Ibrox bosses at that George Young dinner is undetectable. It is doubtful if even the powers of deduction possessed by the pipe-smoking and deerstalkered Sherlock Holmes could have unearthed a satisfactory solution to such a mystery. Perhaps Sir Arthur Conan Doyle, the Edinburgh-born doctor who created that crime-fighting partnership of Holmes and Dr Watson, summed up the case perfectly with these words from his Sherlock Holmes tale, *The Valley of Fear*: "Mediocrity knows nothing higher than itself . . . but talent instantly recognises genius."

George Young simply won't be drawn on the circumstantial evidence surrounding the events of the testimonial, or allow the detailed information to be examined under a microscope, saying only, "For goodness' sake let sleeping dogs lie, Jim, but I will say this . . . nothing can ever erase the memories of those wonderfully happy days which I spent with Glasgow Rangers . . . those memories are very real and they are mine, all mine!"

I can pay no greater personal tribute to the great George Young than to say that I am happy to have lived in his age, proud that he numbers me among his personal friends. Unfortunately, in February 1989, big George suffered a severe stroke and, as if that wasn't enough, had a stomach ulcer removed just a few weeks later. Happily, at the time of writing, "Corky" is well on the road to recovery, thanks mainly to those characteristic fighting qualities and that incomparable spirit. I hope that big, smiling, "lived-in" face of his is with us for a long, long time to come, generating as it does an aura of warmth and friendliness. Had this genial and philanthropic character played but a single game for Cowdenbeath or Lincoln City, he would be deserving of a testimonial. "Gentle Giant", you are a soccer immortal and your place in history is secure. So thanks for the many happy memories, "Captain George". Your countless testimonials, the only kind which really matter in the final analysis, burn like a million candles and can never be extinguished.

Big Geordie Young . . . a genial and philanthropic character!

Because, unlike your narrow-minded and envious critics who, despite their status, understand as little of what football is really all about as a big fellow called Geordie Young knows about the history of table tennis, you truly are . . . the man for all seasons!

For all his attributes, it is as a great player and captain that George will always be remembered. In January 1976, Scotland's manager, the late Willie Ormond, who played against Young on many occasions when a member of Hibernian's fabulous "Famous Five" forward line, said this of big daddy long legs: "George didn't tackle you unnecessarily fiercely, he wasn't too hard on you, he was just fair, firm, clean and deadly accurate . . . George Young of Glasgow Rangers was the most natural captain, the most instinctive leader of men, that I ever encountered in football."

11

THE GOLDEN BOY OF SOCCER

It was six o'clock in the morning. Milk carts were precariously rattling along through an early morning mist and threatening to tumble their jingling cargoes of white bottles all over the narrow streets in the Tees-side town of Redcar. Slowly the doors of a local hotel opened and, after hours of football chit-chat, I emerged woolly-eyed into the eerie light of a new dawn accompanied by that football legend, Wilf Mannion, his wife Bernadette and a few friends.

On the previous day, former Scottish internationalists, George Young of Rangers and John McPhail of Celtic, had journeyed to England's North-East with me as invited guests of The Wilf Mannion and George Hardwick Testimonial Committee . . . and how memorable the occasion honouring those Middlesbrough and England immortals had turned out to be!

The author presents a portrait by Fred Martin to Wilf and Bernadette Mannion on the occasion of the testimonial.

Ironically, John McPhail and I almost missed out on the focal point of those celebrations. Idly chatting in our town-centre hotel while waiting to be bussed to Ayresome Park and the Middlesbrough versus England match, we discovered to our horror that the coaches had left without us and we appeared stranded. But help was on hand, help which materialised from the most unexpected of sources.

"Come on you two, hop on to the bus with the lads," said England manager, Bobby Robson. An admirable gesture indeed . . . but did John McPhail and I really want to be seen on an *English* team bus? Beggars can't be choosers though, so we grabbed the unexpected opportunity and, unbelievably, found ourselves chatting to the players on that luxury coach as it wound its way towards the stadium with fans chanting "England, England" from the roadsides. On arriving at Ayresome Park, we discovered that a large crowd had gathered to welcome the England team. John and I then found ourselves "running the gauntlet" with those English players through a line of police as cheering fans surged forward . . . thank goodness none of those lovely supporters were aware of the fact that big John had played for Scotland and wee Jim was a card-carrying member of the "Tartan Army".

As it transpired the match was a good one . . . with England winning 2–1 and my seat in the director's box next to the Lord Mayor, fully resplendent in his chain of office, was just a little more "up market" than my usual stance on the dear old Easter Road terracing. But, for once, the game itself was relatively unimportant, serving merely as an *hors d'oeuvre* before the feast of football nostalgia which was to follow. It was great to chat at length with Danny Blanchflower and Billy Liddell. How proud I was to be with John and George, who proved marvellous ambassadors for Scotland and kept Middlesbrough manager Malcolm Allison and TV pundit, Jimmy Hill, chuckling with their distinctive brand of Scottish humour.

Wilf Mannion is, of course, a sporting legend in the North-East of England. But the man is much more than just a local hero. For, at the height of his fame, Mannion's name was respected and held in the highest possible esteem throughout the world of football.

Perhaps that oft-quoted character, Bill Shankly, slotted Wilf's talents into perfect perspective when, lavishing praise on Mannion and that other great inside-forward, Ireland's Peter Doherty, "Shanks" said: "When Wilf Mannion or Peter Doherty walk into a room . . . I stand to attention!" And the incomparable Len Shackleton, of Sunderland and England fame, came away with what is, for me, one of football's most imaginative and descriptive quotations when he said: "Wilf could dance on cornflakes without making them crackle . . . he was an artist and a delight to watch!"

Wilfred James Mannion was born on 16 May 1918 in South Bank, a small, tightly knit community nestling on the edge of Middlesbrough. A community that, almost to a man, gleaned a living from the mighty steelworks which, dominating the skyline, were the very lifeblood of Tees-side in the 1920s. Steel, with its jostling ingots and palls of black smoke belching out from towering chimneys which thrust defiantly upwards dissecting a blazing red sky, was the demon King of South Bank. Like great fire-bellied monsters, giant furnaces spewed out ton after ton of white-hot molten steel, spitting millions of dancing sparks into the evening air. Every night was Guy Fawkes Night in South Bank.

Little Wilfred James Mannion, aged only three
. . . complete with whistle and, of course, football!

And those good, honest and hard-working folk, spawned in the rows of grey terraces which clung to the works like limpets, were as tough and durable as that rolled steel itself . . . rolled steel fashioned in what could easily have been mistaken for Hell's kitchen or Satan's base on Earth!

South Bank St Peter's School lay in the heart of this man-made inferno of mayhem. A new school, built in 1924, it could realistically achieve little more than prepare boys for work in those mills with the same, unerring certainty that a miner's lad from a neighbouring Northumberland coalfield would lift a pick and shovel, follow in father's footsteps down into the pit and hew tons of rich black gold from the bowels of an unsympathetic earth, reluctant to yield its treasures.

Wilf Mannion, Middlesbrough and England.

As in all great industrialised communities, football was the burning passion of the lads who grew up in South Bank. The teachers in that little school didn't know it then, but a tiny, golden-haired waif, jinking around the playground with a ball at his feet and mesmerising opponents many years older than himself . . . was to develop into one of the greatest players in the history of soccer!

One of five brothers in a family of ten, Wilf Mannion was honoured by Yorkshire County and won many medals while starring for South Bank St Peter's. But sadly, despite "tearing the opposition to ribbons" in a North versus South international trial match, he was ignored by the English Schoolboy selectors because, at only four feet two inches tall, the lad was deemed too small and frail to merit selection. But such an exceptional soccer talent cannot to be denied indefinitely. That skinny waif's determination to reach the top, coupled with a natural genius which simply can't be taught, provided a sure and certain launching-pad to glory.

Wilf joined the local senior club, Middlesbrough, as a professional in 1936 when seventeen years old. At first he wasn't permitted to train with the other players as it was felt he was too small and slight. But, thanks mainly to the caring attention and encouragement of stars like Billy Forrest, Bobby Baxter as well as manager, Wilf Gillow, he soon gained weight and developed into a much stronger and fitter footballer. After a spell in the reserves, the local lad made his top team debut versus Portsmouth and quickly established himself as a key member of the first eleven.

The Boro' side of the late 1930s was packed with talented players and in that highly-skilled Scot, Benny Yorston, the fair-haired kid found a mentor, a father figure from whom he was to learn many tricks of the trade and eventually succeed. So rapidly did the youngster rocket to stardom that, in March 1938, the highly respected Charlton Athletic manager, Jimmy Seed, was prompted to say of the nineteen-year-old inside-forward: "He is the complete footballer. He cannot get any better."

Wilf aged twelve and honoured by Yorkshire County.

Then, just when young Mannion was beginning to feel on top of the world and playing with tremendous style and confidence, his surge to greatness was cruelly brought to an abrupt halt by the outbreak of war. Drafted into the Green Howards in January 1940, football was relegated to a secondary role, although Wilf was able to keep his eye in playing for the battalion. Just a

Those Dunkirk beaches in 1940 . . . which one is Wilf?

matter of weeks after enlisting, though, he was dispatched to France from a Green Howards' base in Bridlington.

Slicing through Holland, Belgium and Luxembourg like a hot knife through butter, Hitler's Nazi troops crushed the French, forcing that country to sue for armistice. So, rifle in hand, Wilf Mannion, the star footballer, found himself, along with thousands of others, on the beaches at Dunkirk as Britain extricated her army from France and, alone, faced up to the task of repelling the evil scourge of Fascism. Thankfully, although the air bombardment of the United Kingdom continued, Hitler's dream of invading Britain collapsed when the Luftwaffe suffered a crushing defeat in the Battle of Britain.

Wilf (centre) when an infantryman in the Green Howards.

On returning from France Mannion played for Middlesbrough, guested for Spurs as well as Bournemouth and Boscombe and represented England in four wartime international matches versus Scotland before being posted to the Far East and active service in Burma. Far travelled, the South Bank lad was also based in Persia for a spell, appearing in an exhibition match and being introduced to the Shah. Still on the move and never far from the thick of battle, the infantryman next found himself in Sicily. "We had a terrible time there," he says. "Having mounted a night attack on the plains of Catania, close to Mount Etna, we got caught in crossfire and about half of our company of 120 were killed . . . including the man for whom I had acted as runner, Captain Hedley Verity of the Green Howards, the famous Yorkshire and England spin-bowler." From there Wilf crossed the Straits of Messina and advanced northwards from the toe of Italy with the Eighth Army, surviving the battles of Anzio and Casino. Mannion was reported missing but eventually turned up alive and, after contracting malaria, was sent to a convalescent camp in the Middle East before returning home.

Having emerged unscathed from years of frontline active service Mannion is, to this day, philosophical about the "lost" years representing his country in conflicts far removed from those on the football field: "I was lucky, thank God, because, unlike many of my pals, I survived the war when I could so easily have been killed." Following a spell of readjustment and intensive training, Wilf reappeared in the colours of Middlesbrough against Bury on 6 April 1946. Just five months later, Mannion won the first of twenty-six full international caps for England when he played versus Northern Ireland in Belfast. The English lads won 7–2 and Wilf contributed a marvellous hat-trick. "The Dodge" or "Little Fellow", as he was affectionately named, was back in business with a vengeance and there was now no stopping the one who, because of his talents and that crop of fair hair, was also aptly nicknamed "The Golden Boy of Soccer".

The man with the Midas touch starred in many famous England international sides, but perhaps his most notable performance came in a staggering 10–0 win over highly-rated Portugal in Lisbon on 27 May 1947. The inside-forward's name didn't appear on the score-sheet but he helped Tommy Lawton and Stan Mortensen to four apiece and even Matthews to one. Wilf said afterwards: "They changed the ball, they changed the goalkeeper, they changed the backs but it didn't matter what they did, we were completely in charge."

In the same year Mannion "pulled the strings", turned in a fabulous display and scored twice as Great Britain beat the Rest of Europe 6–1 at Hampden Park in a match which marked the return of the British Associations to FIFA and was billed "The Game of the Century". Amazingly, after that performance, the internationally acclaimed star travelled back to Tees-side in the third-class carriage of a packed train. Seated on his suitcase in the corridor, with the cheers of the crowd still ringing in his ears, the hero of Hampden was able to ponder the fact that nobody had even bothered to book him a seat for the journey . . . great players were treated very differently in those days!

Then, in November 1947, the inside-forward played what many regard as his greatest ever game. The mighty Blackpool side were the Ayresome Park visitors and "The Little Fellow", with fiancée Bernadette seated in the stand, turned on a display as sparkling as the diamond on the ring of the love of his life's finger. Sportswriter Cliff Mitchell, who had the good fortune to witness that match, is much better qualified than I to describe the multi-talented forward's display:

The England team which beat Northern Ireland 7–2 in Belfast on 28 September 1946, when Mannion, making his international debut, scored a famous hat-trick. Back row, left to right: Laurie Scott (Arsenal), Neil Franklin (Stoke City), Frank Swift (Manchester City), Billy Wright (Wolves), Henry Cockburn (Manchester Utd). Front row, left to right: Tom Finney (Preston North End), Raich Carter (Derby County), George Hardwick (Middlesbrough, captain), Wilf Mannion (Middlesbrough), Tommy Lawton (Chelsea), Bobby Langton (Blackburn Rovers).

He took the opposition apart, superbly, with style, panache and fantastic skill. He embarked on scything runs. The ball bounced on his head and he allowed it to move down his body, as he still ran, then trapped it before it touched the deck. He moved one way, then the other and, as bemused opponents gave up the ghost, he would send a colleague away in the clear.

Middlesbrough won 4–0 and Mannion's breath-taking exhibition is now part of the folklore of Tees-side. After the match, Blackpool's Stan Mortensen, an outstanding England forward in his own right, had this to say: "When 'The Little Fellow' is in that mood, it's no good trying to do anything about it. He took us apart. He made fools of us. We were backing off in the end. What a performance!"

Matthews and Mannion in training for the 1947 Great Britain versus the Rest of Europe clash . . . and in Scottish tracksuits! If only!

One of Mannion's two goals for Great Britain versus the Rest of Europe in 1947.

Stan Mortensen . . . an outstanding England forward in his own right.

To play twenty-six times for England after his traumatic wartime experiences and at a time when international matches were fewer and competition for places fierce, to say the least, was a staggering achievement. But life was not all a bed of roses for Wilf. Despite his tremendous talents he was restricted to a pre-war maximum wage of £8 in the season and £6 in the summer, which had only risen to £15 and £12 by the time Mannion left Boro' in 1954. Like many of the great players of his time the inside man fell prey to parasites who bled the game of its riches and denied the star players a just return for their efforts . . . and anyone who disagrees with that statement can consider the undeniable fact that second-rate theatre turns were getting *four times* the weekly "silver" that "The Golden Boy" was earning at the zenith of his power. Characteristically, Wilf had the guts to rebel and demand long-term security for his wife and family . . . but, in line with the other clubs, Middlesbrough stuck to the letter of the law.

Disillusioned, the superstar quit football and left his native Tees-side to work for an Oldham company which produced battery systems for rearing poultry. During those troubled times many clubs tried to sign him by offering Middlesbrough FC huge sums of money. Juventus made a move and Celtic manager, Jimmy McGrory, travelled to Tees-side with the staggering offer of £30,000 *plus* the pick of two international players, so eager was he to obtain Mannion's signature. But, like all the others, Mr McGrory was sent packing and Wilf given an ultimatum to go back to Middlesbrough or forget about playing football. Eventually, after nine months in the soccer wilderness, "The Dodge" found himself unable to avoid the inevitable and returned to Ayresome Park. Great though Mannion was, even he was unable to beat the system. Shockingly, many con-men fiddled vast fortunes from football's coffers when grounds were bursting at the seams, while "giants" such as Wilf Mannion were forced to dance to their sordid tune.

But "The Little Fellow's" contribution to football far outweighs that of those who denied him his rights. From all accounts he was a genius, one whose name will forever shine out from the pages of football's story, just as those skies over his native South Bank did when he was a little kid. Those great steel mills built Britain's power and helped win wars. So did Mannion . . . his talents flashed like a beacon across the length and breadth of the Kingdom and, indeed, in every part of the world in which he played—a fact readily substantiated by ex-England team-mates who had a close-up view of "The Golden Boy" at his sparkling best. "What a player! The ball when he moved with it, seemed to be part of him," commented his England inside-forward partner Raich Carter, adding, "He was so easy to play with . . . a natural to

"This is how you do it, lads." Wilf back home in South Bank at the height of his fame
. . . and enjoying a kick-about with some very willing pupils!

end all naturals! I remember when we beat Ireland 7–2. Wilf got a hat-trick. His performance was astounding. There was only one Wilf Mannion!''

Nat Lofthouse, too, has fond memories of ''The Little Fellow'':

I will never forget my first game for England . . . it was at Highbury against Yugoslavia. I was as nervous as a kitten. When I reported to the team hotel I was told that I was sharing a room with Wilf Mannion. I could hardly believe it . . . me with Wilf Mannion! But his jokes soon put me at ease. And, as I lay in the darkness before going to sleep I heard Wilf say from the next bed, ''You'll have a blinder tomorrow, don't worry.'' I got both goals in a 2–2 draw . . . and Wilf made them. He laid on chances for everybody as he always did, I only wish the youngsters of today could see him at his best. When I watched Pele playing I thought of Wilf. Great though Pele was, I am proud to think that I played with as great a player . . . perhaps even greater!

Nat Lofthouse (right) training with the great Tom Finney.

South Bank was, of course, the birthplace of another man of magic, Paul Daniels! Another little fellow who, in common with Mannion, has conjured up endless hours of wonder for millions. Paul has this to say of the footballer who was an ace in every pack with which he played:

Paul Daniels . . that other magician from South Bank!

In a town where all the schoolchildren were trained as fodder for the steelworks in the area, Wilf Mannion was held up as "the one who got away". Chests would swell with pride because he came from our town, and it was one of the precious few things that we had to boast about. Although he played at a time when the rewards were not great, at least he has the knowledge that he played in an era when football was a sport, and not a major commercial enterprise that has somehow lost its family appeal along the way.

In real terms, guys like Wilf Mannion were as big "box office" attractions to football as was John Wayne to the Western movie, Joe Louis to boxing, or Jack Nicklaus to golf—the only difference being that Wilf didn't make a vast fortune through being hailed as a superstar!

The testimonial, which he shared with that fine Middlesbrough and England team-mate, George Hardwick, healed some old wounds and put a few quid into his pocket but, like so many great stars, he was robbed, simply robbed! Incredible though it may seem Mannion has only one memento on display in his Redcar home, a trophy presented by the Priory Club in Middlesbrough on which is inscribed: "To one of the greatest footballers of all time." That says it all. You won your battles, Wilf, all of your battles! For you were "The Golden Boy" when soccer "giants" were abroad and roaming this land in a golden age of football.

Wilf Mannion—the Golden Boy.

12

WHISTLE WHILE YOU WORK

At best he's merely tolerated and, at worst, simply loathed! Yes, our old friend the football referee would play the part of the villain in any movie. More of a Long John Silver than a Jim Hawkins, more akin to the Big Bad Wolf than to Little Red Riding Hood . . . compared to this pathetic apology for a human being, even the evil traffic warden appears as popular as a representative from Littlewood's Pools, who's banging on your front door with a cheque for a million quid plus in his inside pocket!

As far as those football-crazy, knowledgeable and highly articulate lads on the terracings are concerned, that man in black is, unquestionably, the Devil in disguise . . . a damned pest rather than an asset and about as welcome as Count Dracula at the annual Sunday School picnic! Wildly gesticulating and jumping around like some demented fairy while continually getting tangled up with the ball, or, alternatively, lumbering around like Baron Frankenstein's monster and never up with the play . . . he's either got ants in his pants or is about as mobile as an Egyptian mummy. But it's not his mummy who regularly finds herself in the forefront of the fans' minds . . . it's his daddy! Those lads on the terracings are never slow to give vent to their innermost emotions and to express the considered opinion that the identity of the hard-pressed official's father is shrouded in a cloak of mystery. Yes, that b****** of a referee is always obliged to carry a birth certificate around in his top pocket to prove his legitimacy!

Incidentally, there was an occasion when a real Bastard officiated at an important match. Yes, one who rejoiced in the name S.R. Bastard from Upton Park was in charge of the 1877–78 FA Cup final between Wanderers and Royal Engineers and if you don't believe me you can refer to the FA's own publication *We Won the Cup*, which was published in 1971 . . . perhaps it explains the origins of that much-loved and age-old terracing song, *You're a Bastard, Referee*.

The level of appreciation of a referee's skills is minimal and the financial rewards, at best, meagre. So can it be love of the game, dedication above and beyond the call of duty or, more likely, sheer lunacy which makes a man embark on a "career" as a part-time match official? This widely detested and much maligned chappie has walked through more storms than most, trying to hold his head up high but, despite the presence of a pair of linesmen . . . he always walks alone! What inconceivable quirk of human nature could possibly induce a fellow to allow himself to be voluntarily hurled into the gladiatorial arena that is a football field, Saturday after Saturday, season after season, while on all sides rages a hissing, almost hysterical mob, giving him the "thumbs down" and screaming for his blood?

In many respects the lower-ranking match official faces an even more unenviable task. Often having to change in some damp and dingy hut, where he is given the "cold shoulder" and eyed with suspicion by both sets of players, his is a "calling" fraught with danger. Although much smaller in number, a crowd standing around the lines in some public park is just as partisan and, potentially, just as volatile. Nor can the "whistler" who pursues his part-time vocation in such surroundings depend on the "long arm of the law" to reach out and come to his aid should things get out of hand and turn nasty. There is always the distinct possibility that he will have to take to his heels to avoid a ducking in the local pond!

Having miraculously survived the many perils to be confronted in the lower grades of this dreadful "profession", the referee who makes it to the top is likely to find himself bundled on to some aeroplane and heading towards the fearsome prospect of controlling, for instance, an Egypt versus Israel World Cup Qualifying tie. Maybe he'll even be lucky enough to get the opportunity of going sight-seeing behind that Iron Curtain in Albania on some bitterly cold November day. Then, with snow driving into his face and butterflies doing somersaults in his belly, he'll confront the unenviable task and dubious "honour" of controlling proceedings as Albania's much-loved representatives and those of their "friends" from West Germany, square up to each other in an UEFA Cup tie. Language problems don't make the task any easier. Somehow, the petrified official gets the clear impression that the home side's "gorilla" of a central defender isn't exactly enquiring if he is enjoying his stay in their country, while delivering a dose of the verbals and poking a finger deep into the quaking referee's rib cage. Not knowing whether it was the extreme cold or sheer terror which made him shiver like a jelly, having managed to avoid a hail of missiles at the end of the match and been given an armed escort to the airport in the wake of the hostilities, the relieved ref sits on that plane, which departs four hours late, thanking the Lord that he is still in one piece! Not long now and he'll be back in the loving arms of Mary and the kids! However, such blissful peace of mind is short-lived because of the sudden realisation that, two days later, he's scheduled to "run the gauntlet" at the Rangers versus Celtic "Old Firm" match. This quickly brings him back to earth with a thud!

Why, he asks himself, could he not have been more sensible and opted for a more tranquil, rewarding and less hazardous spare-time occupation? Something like a lion tamer or a steeplejack.

Having reared his ugly head for the first time in the late nineteenth century and initially blasted on that damned whistle at a Nottingham Forest versus Sheffield Norfolk match in 1878, the referee is a comparatively modern innovation and our footballing forefathers seemed to get along very nicely without him . . . or did they? Not exactly pleasing to the eye, the cartoon (below/top), which was published around 1830, clearly portrays just what football was really like without the dear old ref. Black eyes, thick ears, bloody noses and broken limbs were the order of the day as an unruly and uncontrolled pack of hooligans without number pursued the bladder with murderous intent.

A hilarious cartoon by H. Heath depicting football as played circa 1830.

Cartoon published by Robert Cruikshank in 1827.

1904 cartoon . . they weren't treated any better in those days!

And the even earlier artist's impression (previous page/bottom) makes one wonder if, all things considered, those kings and queens in the Middle Ages were justified in their efforts to abolish and obliterate the "sport" from the face of the land. So maybe when all is said and done we should be a little more appreciative of the referee's contribution to our national game, demonstrate a bit more compassion and a greater willingness to understand some of the many problems which confront the poor fellow.

It certainly wasn't the milk of human kindness which was dished out to the poor guy (above), depicted in an after-match cartoon from 1904 . . . and the poets too, have frequently been less than kind to the long suffering "whistler":

> At one game the referee
> A silly wee nark,
> Had to flee to the hills
> Until it was dark.
> Then, only then, when darkness came
> Did he come sneakin doon
> And slink awa hame.
>
> (*W.Laurie*)

A certain J.H. Jones, who wrote the following poem for a football paper just after the turn of the century, was also more than a little contemptuous when pouring scorn on the age of referees:

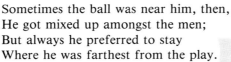

There was a chap who couldn't run,
Whose playing days were long since done;
And consequently he was free
To rule the game as referee.

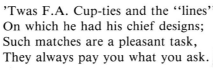

His vision, it must be confessed,
Was scarcely of the very best;
But yet he generally could see
Enough to take his weekly fee.

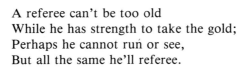

Sometimes the ball was near him, then,
He got mixed up amongst the men;
But always he preferred to stay
Where he was farthest from the play.

'Twas F.A. Cup-ties and the "lines"
On which he had his chief designs;
Such matches are a pleasant task,
They always pay you what you ask.

A referee can't be too old
While he has strength to take the gold;
Perhaps he cannot run or see,
But all the same he'll referee.

A cartoonist's impression of famous Scottish referees in the 1930s.

The following passage is, almost certainly, fictitious, because William Pickford who sponsored it was a famous referee in his own right. However, I'm certain that the vast majority of today's football fans will draw their own modern parallels and readily identify with this derogatory and very humorous description of a whistler's efforts which was first published well over eighty years ago:

Of all the bleary-eyed nincompoops that ever appeared in spindle-shanks on the turf in the guise of a referee, the cachinnatory cough drop who attempted the job on Saturday was the worst we have ever seen. His asinine imbecility was only equalled by his mountebank costume, and his general appearance and get-up reminded one more of a baked frog than a man. No worse tub-thumping, pot-bellied, jerry-built jackass ever tried to perform as a referee. His lugubrious tenebrousness and his monotonous squeaking on the whistle were a trial to the soul. Encased in a dull physiological envelopment of weird chaotic misunderstandings of the rules, he gyrated in a ludicrously painful manner up and down the field, and his addle-headed, flat-chested, splay-footed, cross-eyed, unkempt, unshaven, bow-legged, humpbacked, lop-eared, scraggy, imbecile, and idiotic decision when he ruled Jones' second goal off-side, filled the audience, players and spectators alike, with disgust.

In the 1860s and 1870s the referee sat on the sidelines while two umpires, one in each half, made the on-field decisions, the referee only being consulted should those umpires fail to agree. Although invested with greater powers in 1889, it was not until 1891 that the dear old ref, complete with notebook and whistle, was transferred from the touchline to take control of events within

That two refs experiment at the Amateur International trial played at Chester in 1935. The referees, Dr A.W. Barton (left) and E. Wood (right) are here seen supervising the toss.

the playing area. Those umpires were then demoted to linesmen, their main function being to indicate when the ball went out of play. In the mid-1930s the Football Association actually considered turning the clock back by abolishing those linesmen altogether and placing a referee in charge of each half of the field. This crazy notion was put to the test in two 1935 trial games, the first occasion being the Amateur International trial match at Chester on 5 January and the second an International trial played at West Bromwich on 27 March.

What a chilling thought . . . two referees! My God, are things not bad enough with one? It is hard to imagine the confusion which would ensue were two of those authoritarian blighters let loose on the same field. Thankfully that 1935 proposition was widely condemned by the clubs and quickly consigned to the FA dustbin.

Those social outcasts in black, like tax inspectors, are not exactly my favourite group of individuals and, maybe, after all the abuse which I have hurled at them in my time, it is more than a little hypocritical to find myself championing the cause of football's most detested participants. But, although they are never likely to figure on many Xmas card lists, just for once, let's look at things from the ref's viewpoint!

'Where to, ref? . . . The station?' (By courtesy of Punch*).*

For a start he's paid a mere pittance for risking life and limb. The poor man is subjected to constant scrutiny by eagle-eyed referee supervisors and is frequently mercilessly lambasted by biased football managers and the unsympathetic gentlemen of the sporting press . . . with absolutely no right of reply! While our friend the referee spends what is left of a nail-biting weekend writing his match report or studying the complex and ever-changing rules which he has to know like the back of his hand, those jet-setting players are hitting the high spots and enjoying the adoration of their devoted fans. Then, come Monday morning, while our much-maligned match official is grounded and hard at work in that bank or factory where he is being subjected to yet another inquisition by sneering colleagues who have analysed his performance on TV and read the highly critical comments in the press . . . with bonus money almost bursting their wallets, the players of Newton United are winging their way to a well-earned week of luxury in sunny Spain, which is their reward for finishing third bottom of the league and keeping their second-rate club in the first division.

So next time you feel inclined to hurl a deluge of foul-mouthed abuse at the poor old referee, or to question the identity of his paternal parent, pause for a moment and try to imagine just what football was really like without him. To be realistic, there is absolutely no chance of the match official getting the red card or being forced to swallow that damned whistle of his, so we'll just have to learn how to coexist with him, won't we? Although nauseating and extremely difficult to stomach, the fact is that football owes a considerable debt of gratitude to that very special breed of sad and lonely men who, despite suffering dogs' abuse and being subjected to terrible torment, whistle while they work in an admirable effort to ensure that fair play is observed at all times.

13

THE SHUT-OUT KINGS OF WEMBLEY

It takes a very special type of courage to scale the terrifying heights of Everest or to take Man's first faltering footsteps on the surface of the moon. Human beings have always striven to push themselves to the very limits of endurance and to confront the gravest of dangers in their quest to conquer seemingly impossible goals. In the football world there can be no more frightening or awe-inspiring business than to wear the Scottish international goalkeeper's jersey at Wembley, because Scotland's record beneath those famous twin towers is, at best, a chequered one!

It is with profound emotion and inestimable pride that folk born north of the Tweed recall the exploits of the legendary "Wembley Wizards". That 5–1 Scottish victory, on 31 March 1928, was probably Scottish international football's finest hour (and a half). But in all honesty it is the goalscoring feats of those white-shirted English lads which have made the biggest and most significant impact on the battles between the Thistle and the Rose at the high altar of English football. The very mention of names like Cliff Bastin, Nat Lofthouse, Johnny Haynes, Bobby Charlton and Kevin Keegan sends a cold shiver down the spines of Scottish football enthusiasts because, whispering across the decades, comes the chilling fact that an avalanche of English goals has turned Wembley into a nightmare arena for many a Scottish goalkeeper.

In 1955, for instance, Freddie Martin of Aberdeen retrieved the ball from the back of the Scottish net seven times as Denis Wilshaw of Wolves helped himself to a record four goals in England's 7–2 win. And, if those "Wizards" provided the Scottish game with its most famous international triumph, then surely England's 9–3 victory in 1961 was Scotland's blackest day. Jimmy Greaves (three), Johnny Haynes (two), Bobby Smith (two), Bryan Douglas and that England manager, Bobby Robson, scored the goals which numbed a nation and saw goalkeeper Frank Haffey, his team-mates and the heart-broken "Tartan Army" sounding a hasty retreat and scurrying northwards with those Lion Rampants fluttering limply at half-mast.

Jimmy Greaves scores one of his hat-trick as England crush the Scots in 1961.

It's a sad fact that great Scottish goalies of the calibre of Jack Harkness, John Jackson, Jimmy Cowan, Tommy Younger and Bill Brown have all failed to keep their goal intact at wonderful Wembley. Indeed, in the twenty-eight full international fixtures (up to and including the 1988 match) played at the stadium since England and Scotland drew 1–1 in Wembley's first ever international on 12 April 1924, Scotland has selected twenty-one different men to play in the last line of her defence and, amazingly, only two have achieved a Wembley shut-out. Dave Cumming of Middlesbrough in 1938, when the Scots won 1–0 and Alan Rough, then of Partick Thistle, who played in the Scottish side which won by the same scoreline in 1981, are the men who share this rare honour.

Furthermore, since the Scots first played a full international match on English soil at Kennington Oval in 1873, only four Scottish goalkeepers have prevented England from scoring at home in an official match, the others being Kenneth Campbell of Partick Thistle in 1922 at Villa Park and Willie Harper of Arsenal in 1926 at Old Trafford. Coincidentally, Scotland won both of

Those shut-out Kings of Wembley . . . Dave Cumming (left) and Alan Rough.

those matches 1–0. On his fourth Wembley appearance that great Glasgow Rangers 'keeper, Jerry Dawson, played in a Scottish side which drew 0–0 on 10 October 1942 but of course that was a wartime match and is classified as unofficial.

When Dave Cumming and Alan Rough met for the first time two or three years ago they were, until then, totally unaware of the honoured place which they share in Scottish football's "Hall of Fame". "It would seem that ours is a very exclusive club, Alan," quipped Dave. "Yes," replied "Roughie". "We really could hold our AGM in a phone box."

Dave Cumming's fingers are gnarled and twisted, a lasting and painful reminder of his playing days but, in characteristic fashion, Dave doesn't complain. "In those days we didn't play with a balloon like you do, Alan," he joked. "Handling and clearing that heavy, old-fashioned ball could be a painful business when you didn't connect properly. I was forever breaking and dislocating my fingers and, let's face it, the rules of the game weren't designed to protect goalkeepers in my day," added Dave. "Ah, but that so-called balloon bends and dips more readily and moves much faster . . . doesn't it Dave?'' retorted Alan. Dave simply gave a knowing smile and those two placid and likeable men went their separate ways in total agreement that whatever era they played in, theirs was the craziest and most thankless of vocations.

I am reminded of an occasion when I visited "Wembley Wizard" goalkeeper, Jack Harkness, in his Glasgow home. Jack was a great and widely respected character, whose description of a typical example of the perils which confronted a goalkeeper in his time, left a lasting impression on my mind.

Jack Harkness.

"Imagine going up to collect that heavy, sodden ball on a wet day, certain that, at the very instant you lay hands on the leather, the powerful 'Dixie' Dean, who's been steaming in from some unknown direction, is going to wallop you like an express train and attempt to knock you into the back of the net with the ball," said Jack, adding: "My body shook right down to my boots and it was all that I could do to withstand the impact and, at the same time, keep my hands on the ball."

Unlike Alan Rough, Dave Cumming played senior football on both sides of the border. The goalkeeper joined Aberdeen in 1930 and also played for Arbroath before being signed by Middlesbrough for a £3,000 fee in October 1936. Cumming's 1938 Wembley stint was his only full international appearance, while, at the time of writing, Rough is Scotland's most-capped goalkeeper, having represented his country on no fewer than fifty-three occasions.

Despite the fact that Dave Cumming and Alan Rough are the only Scottish goalkeepers to achieve a shut-out in a full international match at Wembley, both men have experienced the agony and anguish of retrieving the ball from the back of the Scottish net at the Empire Stadium. Alan played in Scotland's 2–1 victory in 1977 and in the Scottish side which lost by the same scoreline in 1986 and, although it was in a wartime international, Dave was the fellow unfortunate enough to find himself between those Scottish goalposts when England trounced the Scots 6–2 on 14 October 1944.

On 8 March 1873, Robert Gardner of Queen's Park became the first Scottish goalie to represent his country south of the border in a full international match. Since, and including, that game which England won 4–2, thirty-seven different goalkeepers have worn old Caledonia's colours in the fifty-three full international contests staged on the English side of the Cheviot Hills. Although virtually all of those men were household names and had climbed to the very summit of their chosen profession, not one ended his playing career without experiencing the trauma of conceding at least one international goal in the land of the Saxons! Even when the 2–2 draw in the Victory International, played at Goodison Park, Liverpool on 26 April 1919 and the nine wartime internationals played in England between 1939 and 1945 are taken into account, the depressing fact from a Scottish viewpoint is that no Scottish goalkeeper has ended his playing career with a completely clean sheet on English soil—a fact which will, doubtless, bring a smug smile of satisfaction to the familiar features of television football pundit, Jimmy Greaves.

Naturally we Scots don't share Greavsie's often-expressed opinion that the standard of Scottish goalkeepers leaves a lot to be desired when compared with their English counterparts. But, if we're honest, we really do have to admit that Jimmy is more than a little qualified to comment and pass judgement, because it's doubtful if British football ever produced a sharper or more natural goal-grabber than the darting and deadly ex-England star. Former Scotland goalkeeper, Frank Haffey, who found himself on the wrong end of that Greaves hat-trick in 1961, would be the first to concede that football's version of the "Crafty Cockney" certainly knew how to hit the target!

But let's be fair, Jimmy . . . even characters like you should show a little sympathy for guys such as Fred Martin and big Frank Haffey, because it isn't always the goalie's fault, is it? And, while you're at it, spare at least a passing thought for poor old Joe Crozier of Brentford who, in the two wartime internationals played in England in which he figured, conceded fourteen goals. You can imagine how bad the Scottish side must have been or, conversely, how well the English lads must have played, when Joe was hailed as a "hero" in the press after Scotland had been thrashed 8–0 at Maine Road, Manchester

Jimmy Greaves . . . football's version of darts champ,
Eric Bristow, ''The Crafty Cockney''.

on 16 October 1943. Four months later, on 19 February 1944, poor Joe was back in the Scottish goal and this time England won 6–2 at Wembley. I'll bet he was pleased that other, more important, battles being waged across Europe at the time quickly pushed football to the back of the public mind. Crozier couldn't have been sorry that those wartime clashes avoided the huge glare

Joe Crozier . . . the ''hero'' who conceded fourteen goals!

of publicity which they would have attracted in peacetime and the unfortunate fellow must have been further relieved to see those internationals consigned to the unofficial category.

Dave Cumming describes goalies as "the most helpless and pathetic guys on Earth". It's easy to understand why he has come to that conclusion when you consider that Dave had to pit his wits against many of soccer's greatest goalscorers, including the legendary Jimmy McGrory of Celtic. "I remember an occasion when playing for Arbroath against the Celts," says Dave. "The

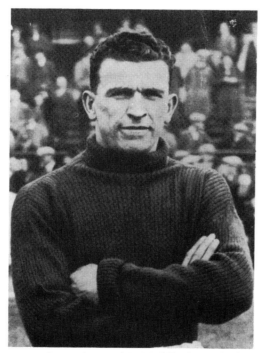

Dave Cumming in his Middlesbrough days.

ball was just inside the penalty area and a crowd of players were scrambling for it. While I was watching everybody's feet I caught a glimpse of the ball and then saw it about two feet from the ground. Suddenly something which looked like a plane in a power dive came into the picture. Jimmy McGrory had hurled himself at the ball and completely fooled me with his diving header when the worst I was expecting was a shot.

Dave visibly winces when he casts his mind back all those years to that other great player who was renowned for his exceptional heading ability. "This fellow wore the blue shirt of Everton and the white shirt of England,'' says Cumming. ''When 'Dixie' Dean's head was in action all any 'keeper could do was stand, watch, hope and wonder how he did it. A flick of his head would have you running so far in the wrong direction that when you stopped you'd be likely to find yourself in the middle of the local High Street. He could fool goalies more easily with a shake of that famous head than any sleight-of-hand merchant could with a hat which produced elephants.

''In my day there were many great sharpshooters who could bamboozle goalkeepers with all kinds of tricks'', adds Dave. ''I used to dream of getting revenge on guys like McGrory, Dean, Ted Drake, George Stevenson and Cliff Bastin. They'd be stuck in the goal while I played the same tricks on them and left those pathetic individuals standing like fools in a net bulging with balls I had put there . . . then I'd fall out of bed and realise that all dreams must end.''

Goalkeepers are certainly an extremely brave and unique breed of men, especially the Scottish variety who are unlucky enough to be selected to represent their country at Wembley. Thankfully I will never be put in the position but, personally speaking, I'd rather try to survive for fifteen rounds in a boxing ring with Rocky Marciano at the height of his fame or attempt to negotiate the Grand National course at Aintree on one of those donkeys from Blackpool beach, than be dragged kicking and screaming only to be planted under that Scottish crossbar at the soccer home of the ''Sassenachs''.

Dave Cumming and Alan Rough are, indeed, members of one of football's most exclusive clubs . . . a club which is simply crying out for new blood! I take my tammie off to those two great characters and to the next brave fellow who, although he should be put in a strait-jacket, will attempt to emulate them in taking the long and lonely walk on to the lush green grass of Wembley. That tammie will be thrown high in the air if some future custodian of the Scottish goal achieves a shut-out on his debut at the capital of English football and, should that ever happen, I would strongly advise the unknown hero to make absolutely certain that he never wears an international jersey beneath those twin towers again. However strong the inclination may be to repeat the remarkable feat, he must give the graveyard of Scottish goalkeepers a very wide berth and, if he has the good sense to listen to that advice, he will indeed hold a unique distinction in the long and—sometimes—glorious history of Scottish football.

Alan Rough.

14

I HAVE A DREAM

You'd hardly think so nowadays but, when all is said and done, the *only* people who really matter when it comes to football are the players and the fans! They go together like coffee and cream, like Laurel and Hardy, like love and marriage. Managers, media men and administrators are purely hod-carriers, because the players are the skilled bricklayers and the supporters the unshakeable mortar. Together they form the very foundations on which soccer is built. Others may greedily hog the limelight and lay claim to being the architects of the modern game, but without those essential building components their empires would be constructed on ever-shifting sands . . . and they should *never* be allowed to forget that!

It has long been my contention that the players and fans must play a much more significant part in controlling the game. Why should self-appointed committees of fuddy-duddies dictate the overall policies and regulations which pertain to football? The players and fans should jointly flex their muscles, exert their considerable potential for power and *demand* a much greater say in the running of the game. Club and association chiefs should, if they fail to measure up, be held accountable for their actions, and, if neces-sary, be presented with the Grand Order of the Boot by a much more democratic and widely representative body than exists at present. There is no other branch of the entertainment industry, including sport, in which direc-tors and managers adopt such a high media profile. Why do so many media men always seem to imagine that fans want to hear endless opinions expressed by the club chairman or manager? I'm pretty certain that the football-loving public would much rather listen to the voice of the players.

Early in 1987 Halifax Town found themselves hovering on the brink of extinction and appealed to Calderdale Council to bale them out of their finan-cial crisis. Councillor David Helliwell, a lifelong Town supporter, persuaded the council to stump up £400,000 to clear club debts and buy back the 125-year lease on the ground, The Shay. Helliwell's vision flies in the face of traditional and outmoded styles of club ownership. "Everyone assumes football clubs have to be run by directors who are local businessmen. Why?" says Helliwell. "The commercial model of clubs run by the butcher, the baker and the candlestick maker has been a disaster, even on its own terms . . . eighty of the ninety-two League clubs in England are insolvent! Boardrooms are full of chancers and ego-trippers. Why should they alone decide the fate of something with which whole communities identify? All the expertise you need to run a football club exists within a local authority." I wish Halifax Town well and will monitor their progress with considerable interest.

But, whoever pulls the strings, soccer represents a way of life for millions, a game which embodies their dreams and grips their emotions. To friends overseas (at least the ones I know) memories of my homeland are infinitely more likely to reverberate around past achievements of the favourite team, than are visions of *Granny Hielan' Hame* or *The Bonnie, Bonnie Banks o' Loch Lomond*. Those soccer-starved exiles are much more inclined to select their reading material from the football bookshelves than to become immersed in the works of Shakespeare, Browning or Keats, however admirable. The White Cliffs of Dover, Morris dancing round the maypole and trooping the colour in the Mall never even cross the mind as fond recollections of the towering grandstands at the likes of Goodison Park in Liverpool or Maine Road in Manchester, standing majestically amid those smoking chimneys on top of row upon row of Coronation Streets, bring a lump to the throat and a tear to the eye!

Closer to home, Bob Laird is a football fan whose cherished memories of his beloved Third Lanark live on, despite the fact that the "Hi-Hi" folded over twenty years ago, in 1967. A former ball boy and programme seller at Third Lanark's Cathkin Park, Bob has built up a fitting memorial to the famous Glasgow club in his East Kilbride home. Programmes, books, piles of old photographs and even bricks from the demolished Cathkin stand and pavilion can be found among his treasured souvenirs.

Over the years Bob Laird has mounted many free exhibitions, part of a personal crusade aimed at keeping the name of his favourite club alive. It is very much a labour of love with absolutely no element of commercial gain. An admirable, "never say die" type of character, the man's enthusiasm is infectious. He reverently rattles off the names of Third's legends of long ago, such as Jimmy Brownlie, Jimmy Mason and Dave Hilley, as if they were still thrilling the fans on those historic slopes of Cathkin Park.

Bob's bricks are lasting reminders of the ground where he spent much of his childhood. When Cathkin was being razed to the ground, the Third Lanark archivist was busily rummaging through the rubble, searching for a couple of undamaged bricks to add to his collection. Suddenly and without warning, he was stopped in his tracks. A sharp-eyed representative from within the ranks of Her Majesty's law enforcement officers, known locally as the "Glesga Polis", had spotted the intrepid souvenir hunter. No doubt the policeman had been observing Bob's actions with profound suspicion and had come to the conclusion that he was a looter. Quickly grabbing a couple of bricks, young Laird fled from the scene of his "crime", hotly pursued by the constable. Happily Bob managed to evade the lawman's clutches, thereby avoiding the embarrassment of being forced to explain his actions. So, to this

Bob Laird in a corner of his "Hi Hi" museum.

very day, a little part of dear old Cathkin can be found in a Third Lanark museum tucked away in a room of Bob's home, among the thousands of houses which make up the sprawling maze that is the township of East Kilbride.

Not quite so admirable but, nevertheless, very likeable were three Celtic supporters whom I met on a Lisbon-bound plane in 1967. Tom, a man in his early fifties, and sons, Tony and John, who would be about twenty and nineteen respectively, were part of an invasion force of some 10,000 Celtic fans heading for the Portuguese capital desperately hoping that the Glasgow side would become the first British club to win the European Cup. To cut a long story short, I arrived in Lisbon with these new pals to find the city awash with Celtic followers who danced, bathed in the local fountains and endeared themselves to the dusky citizens with their boisterous, but good-humoured, antics.

It has to be admitted that Tom, his sons and I enjoyed a few beers in the Lisbon sunshine as we contentedly wandered from hostelry to hostelry, sampling the local brew and soaking in the atmosphere—a pattern interrupted for only a brief spell when my friends decided to visit the nearest chapel and pray for victory. Not being a Roman Catholic and only an adopted Celtic supporter for the day, I respectfully declined their kind offer to accompany them and arranged to team up with the lads half an hour later. However, overcome with curiosity, I secretly followed those devoted fans to their place of worship and, keeking round the door, was highly amused to observe that one side of the church was packed with Celtic followers wearing their green and white colours, while the other side was full of opposing Inter Milan supporters, clad in the black and blue of the Italian champions. Without wishing to appear in any way disrespectful, I suppose it was a case of "make-your-mind-up time" as far as God was concerned!

When the hour finally arrived for us to board the bus which would transport our merry gang the several miles from the centre of Lisbon to the stadium, Tom was, to put it mildly, suffering from the effects of alcohol. Or, to be blunt, he was as p***** as a proverbial newt. "What are we going to do with your dad?" I asked the boys. Pondering the dilemma for a moment, then turning to his brother, the older lad said in a very matter of fact manner, "Why don't we roll the old b****** under this bush and we'll pick him up efter the gemme?" The younger brother nodded in agreement and they proceeded to abandon their legless father under some shrubbery in the centre of a city thousands of miles from home.

Unable to believe what was happening, nor begin to contemplate such a solution to our predicament, I insisted that whatever else happened "Pop" was staying with us. His sons, somewhat reluctantly, agreed, helped me drag the prostrate figure of their father on to that bus, and we duly headed for the match. As the history books record, Celtic beat Inter Milan 2–1 and thousands of delirious Scots danced on the Portuguese pitch, while Tom, as he had done throughout the entire game, lay sound asleep on the terracing! No doubt, when back home in Glasgow and seated in his usual corner of the local pub, the bold boy would be proclaiming, as Welsh comedian, Max Boyce, would put it, ''I know 'cos I was there'', when describing Celtic's famous victory down to the very last detail.

In happier times there was no more spectacular or good-natured football occasion than Scotland's biennial trip to Wembley. Win or lose the ''Tartan Army'' took the capital by storm in a cavalcade of colour. But, the battle o'er and the skirl of the pipes faded into the memory, some of those Scottish invaders had to ''face the music'' after a ''Highland fling'' in the Metropolis.

Trafalgar Square 1977 . . . and the presentation of a Scottish banner to Lord Nelson by the ''Tartan Army''.

Come Monday morning, magistrates in the London courts could expect a queue of Scots accused of minor offences such as breach of the peace or drunk and disorderly behaviour. On one occasion a magistrate was busily dishing out small fines when a kilted Glaswegian appeared before him to answer for some boisterous antics in Trafalgar Square on the Saturday evening. Within minutes the Scot was found guilty. "Have you anything to say before I fine you £10?" asked the magistrate. "Yes, my Lord," replied the Glasgow lad. "Would it be regarded as contempt of court if I was to describe your Honour as a daft old b******?" Hardly believing his ears the irate magistrate roared angrily, "It most certainly would, my man." And, sporting a broad grin, the cocky wee Scot said, "In that case I'll no bother then." Typical Glasgow humour, but it earned the impertinent individual a hefty fine and more time spent in the cells.

This fan has derived great pleasure from having been afforded the privilege of conversing with many of the great soccer stars of the past. The limitations which space imposes don't allow me to include as many tales from their memoirs as I would wish to within the pages of this book. But Tom "Tiny" Bradshaw, Matt Armstrong and Allan Craig are players from bygone days whose inclusion is of the utmost importance to me.

Tom "Tiny" Bradshaw pictured in his Bury days.

Bradshaw played for Scotland just once, but his international cap was won in the greatest Scottish victory of all time! Although born in Bishopton, Renfrewshire, Tommy spent his formative years in the Lanarkshire town of Coatbridge. He played for the strangely-named Woodside Weeps before Coatbridge man, Billy "Kiltie" Cameron, then manager of English Second Division club, Bury, persuaded the massive eighteen-year-old defender to join the Lancashire club in July 1922. Big Tommy helped Bury win promotion the following season and spent nearly eight happy years at Gigg Lane before an £8,000 transfer made him a Liverpool player in January 1930. "Tiny" spent a further eight years at Anfield, during which time he captained the club and, demonstrating remarkable ball control for his size, established himself as one of the top centre-halves in the English First Division. Bradshaw, a key figure in the heart of the Scottish defence when those "Wembley Wizards" hammered England 5–1 in 1928, always made light of his own contribution to that famous victory:

> I had the best view in the ground, Jim, and I got in for nothing. I just stood there and watched Alec Jackson get a hat-trick and Alex James score twice. The whole game hinged on our move after English left-winger Smith hit a great shot against the post early on, and Jimmy McMullan sent Alan Morton away with a pass from the rebound. Alan lobbed the ball over and Jackson headed home. I'll never forget the beauty of the soccer our forwards played from then on to score four more. That forward-line of Jackson, Jimmy Dunn, Hughie Gallacher, James and Morton was the real "Wizard" of Wembley . . . Scotland could have won by ten or more goals had they concentrated on putting the ball into the back of the net, instead of teasing and tormenting that English defence when we were well ahead.

Despite his modesty, the truth of the matter is that Tommy held the Scottish rear-guard together in the early stages of the match when the English forwards had threatened to run riot. Astonishingly Bradshaw was promptly forgotten by the selectors and was the only "Wizard" to gain just one cap, mainly due to the fact that the great Davie Meiklejohn of Glasgow Rangers was automatic choice for the centre-half position in that era.

On several occasions I had the great pleasure of talking to Tommy in his Coatbridge home, and the last survivor of those "Wembley Wizards" always made me most welcome. "Tiny" was a fine big fellow who gleefully grabbed any opportunity to talk about his playing days. On one occasion I visited him with Bobby Flavell, himself a Scottish internationalist. Bobby and I were saddened to notice that Tommy had safety pins keeping his trouser legs together.

He looked a poor soul, not because the big man had been anything other than sensible throughout his life but, quite simply, because he was old, lonely and virtually forgotten. Tommy fumbled through a pile of vintage, dog-eared photographs and passed them to Bobby and me in turn, while reflecting on a happier period in his life. Handing us a picture in which he was leading Liverpool out for a derby match, with the legendary "Dixie" Dean of Everton beside him, "Tiny" commented: "Dixie and I had some tremendous battles in the 1920s and 1930s . . . I can tell you!" Glancing down at the photograph once again, then looking up at the smiling, wizened old face of Tommy Bradshaw, Bobby Flavell said, "Aye, Tommy . . . and you were a really good-looking big lad then." Grinning broadly while rolling those false teeth around in his mouth, the old boy looked over at me, winked and replied, "What do you mean *were*, Bobby . . . what do you mean *were*, you cheeky little monkey!"

The epitome of good nature, big Tommy was a gentle man who was much loved and respected by each and every one of his football contemporaries. Needless to say, when big "Tiny" was buried in the local Coatbridge cemetery in February 1986, Bobby Flavell and I couldn't help but notice that the clubs he had served so well and football's hierarchy were conspicuously absent . . . not represented at the funeral of the last of those "Wembley Wizards", a good and faithful old servant and, undeniably, a very special

Matt Armstrong (left) and Willie Mills in the pre-war black and gold of Aberdeen.

character. Tommy once said to me: "Look into a man's eyes when he is talking about football and you can tell how much he loves the game. Remember, Jim, the eyes speak louder than the tongue . . . watch the eyes, son, watch the eyes!" Sound advice from the great Tommy Bradshaw, a man whom I will never forget.

Nor will I ever forget Matt Armstrong, a prolific goal-scorer for Aberdeen Football Club in the 1930s, who is a character out of football's very top drawer. The former centre-forward played three times for Scotland in full international matches when competition for places was fierce and such honours were very hard to come by. I couldn't count the hours which Matt and I spent blethering on the telephone while the bills mounted . . . no prizes for guessing what was the sole topic of conversation! A wonderful and widely respected player, Matt's club partnership with inside-forward, Willie Mills, is reputed to have bordered on the telepathic. Without question, Matt and Willie were the "northern lights" of old Aberdeen. Were they still playing today they would be absolutely priceless!

Matt has become a great friend of our family and I have a deep regard and affection for the man. Unfortunately he is now resident in Aberdeen's City Hospital, just a matter of yards from the scene of his many triumphs at Pittodrie Stadium, and those twice-weekly phone calls are, sadly, a thing of the past. There is much which could be said of Matt Armstrong but, unfortunately, I am restricted to a few lines as the pages of this book dwindle to a precious few. There is, however, one little tale which must be told and which best describes the character and personality of the man.

For some time I had been trying to trace Scottish internationalist, Andy Black, who played for Hearts, Manchester City and Stockport County between 1934 and 1953. In the course of conversation I asked Matt if he had any clue as to Andy's whereabouts. He didn't. But after describing Black's talents as a forward in glowing terms and telling me repeatedly what a nice fellow Andy was, Matt said, "Listen, Hearts are at Pittodrie tomorrow, so I'll nip down early, meet the team bus, talk to the Hearts people and find out where Andy is now." Matt was unwell at the time and I told him not to bother, especially as it was late November and I didn't relish the thought of him standing in the cold. Typically, he refused to take no for an answer and I reluctantly agreed to phone him the following evening. "You'll never guess what happened Jim," said Matt when I called. "I was waiting for ages but finally the Hearts bus arrived and I asked one of the directors if he had any idea where Andy Black could be contacted. Do you know what he said, Jim? Do you know what the blighter said? You won't believe this but he said, 'I've never even heard of Andy Black'."

The author flanked by those "northern lights" of old Aberdeen, Matt Armstrong (left) and Willie Mills.

Well, that was tantamount to throwing a bright red Aberdeen strip on to the horns of a raging bull. Matt rounded on the unfortunate director, telling him in no uncertain terms that, if he had never heard of a great Hearts player like Andy Black, he had absolutely no right to be a director of such a fine club. That incident greatly angered and depressed the old boy and his anger was justified.

Another unforgettable occasion was when I visited former Motherwell, Chelsea and Scotland centre-half, Allan Craig. In the geriatric ward of a Paisley hospital just weeks before he died, Allan told me about an incident which had marred his life.

Motherwell were leading Celtic 2–1 with just seconds remaining of the 1931 Scottish Cup Final, when Craig headed a tragic own goal to level the scores and earn Celtic a replay. Tears flooding from his eyes, the luckless Craig fell to the ground rolling over and over in mental agony. Before Allan could recover his composure the full-time whistle blew and, while celebrating Celtic fans invaded the pitch mobbing their favourites, the Motherwell defender walked slowly and sorrowfully from the scene of a personal disaster. Heart-broken, the big fellow headed straight back to his native Paisley after the

Allan Craig in Chelsea's colours.

match and spent that Saturday evening sitting alone on a bench in the local park. He knew in his heart that Motherwell's chances of winning the Scottish Cup for the first time had gone. As expected, Celtic duly won 4–2 in the replay and, although Allan had the consolation of winning a League championship medal with the "Steelmen" in 1932, the big centre-half felt relieved to put a few hundred miles between himself and the scene of that nightmare when packing his bags and heading south to join Chelsea for a £4,000 fee in January 1933.

To sit in a hospital ward while an old man grips your hand and, fighting back the tears, recalls a personal nightmare which happened well over half a century earlier, was a very moving experience. One fleeting moment of misfortune had blighted his entire life, because Craig felt wholly responsible for the fact that his team-mates had been denied a coveted Scottish Cup winner's medal. Big Allan bore that heavy burden of personal guilt on his broad shoulders for over fifty years and tearfully took it with him to his grave . . . such is the power and impact that this all-absorbing game which they call football can have on the lives of those who operate within its considerable shadow.

Human beings are, ostensibly, historical manuscripts . . . books which walk, or hobble in the case of ex-footballers, and far too many fine players have passed away without being afforded the opportunity of recording their story for posterity. Sadly, when that shrill sound of life's full-time whistle echoes in their ears, the most that many of those stars of the past can expect by way of tribute to their volume of achievements are a few lines tucked away in the obituary columns of their local paper.

> When I was young and played the game,
> And happy crowds did shout my name,
> The greatest I would always be,
> But now, no one remembers me!
> I jinked and danced and scored and ran,
> A hero loved by every fan,
> My skills, to me, they brought such fame,
> But now so few recall my name!
>
> And now I'm done and soon I'll dee,
> O'er life's long road I've striven,
> . . . I know just who'll remember me!
> . . . My old team-mates in Heaven!
> Tho' maybe I'll gang doon tae Hell,
> And then, how would I feel?
> . . . My fitba' stories I'd just tell,
> While dribblin' roon the De'il!

Football has never been treated more seriously than it is today . . . and that's a great pity! Fear of the consequences of losing has led to an over-emphasis on the negative aspects of the playing side of the game. Consequently a generation has grown up having been denied the right to witness football as it should really be played. Apart from a few notable exceptions, the current generation of soccer fans have to be content with an over-indulgence in physical effort and a "get behind the ball in numbers" philosophy which have widely replaced ball-playing skills in a sport which at one time had much more to offer in terms of entertainment value. The prime objective of football should surely be to entertain the paying public and, in doing so, to put the ball into the back of the opposition net as many times as possible. All too often teams take the field with the paramount aim of preventing the other side from scoring . . . a dreadful situation which, in my opinion, could be partially resolved by awarding four points for a win, two for a score draw, one for a non-scoring draw and, of course, none for a defeat!

Sadly missing from today's soccer scenario are the significant numbers of characters who, once upon a glorious time, introduced a sense of fun and an element of eccentricity to the finest game devised by Man. In this world, where an acceptable level of mediocrity is the order of the day, there would appear to be little or no niche for the oddity, and that is sad. It's all too easy to blame television, hooliganism and high levels of unemployment for football's ailments. Perhaps the most likely diagnosis lies in the fact that there are no longer any Jackie Milburns "thieving" countless goals for those "Magpies" at St James's Park in Newcastle . . . no Charlie Cookes "tripping the light fantastic" and setting fans singing through the wind and rain at Chelsea's Stamford Bridge . . . no Bests, Laws or Charltons "dancing" on the sacred turf of Old Trafford and raising clenched fists of victory to those lads in the Stretford End . . . no Geoff Hursts or Bobby Moores delicately blowing bubbles into the night air at West Ham's Upton Park . . . no Johnny MacKenzies "flying" down that Firhill right wing in the red and yellow of those "Maryhill Magyars", dear old Partick Thistle! . . . no stars such as Stan Matthews, Stan Mortensen or Jackie Mudie making Bloomfield Road's version of the Blackpool illuminations light up the dullest of October days . . . no Finneys at Deepdale, Mannions at Ayresome, Shackletons at Roker or John Whites "ghosting" past the stoutest of defences at mighty Tottenham's White Hart Lane. Could that, I ask myself, be the real reason?

Each generation looks back with affection on the exploits of the great players who brightened childhood. Perhaps distance does lend enchantment and we do tend to exaggerate the abilities of our heroes. Football in the 1950s left a lasting impression on my mind and, obviously, I regard that as being a golden age of the game. Yet, in a poem called *The Mystery of the Missing Millions*, published in the 1956/57 edition of the *FA Year Book*, Cyril Hughes delightfully expresses the opinion that, even then, things were not as they had once been.

> The game that made illustrious a host of famous names,
> From Bloomer, Chambers, Meredith, to Cresswell, Dean and James,
> Now gained in speed and recklessness, but lost in style and skill,
> As craft gave way to earnestness, and genius to will.
> On fields that artists lately trod, apprentices did roam;
> And everybody wondered why spectators stayed at home.
>
> The ball by now was in the air as much as on the ground,
> And while they waited for its fall, the players rushed around
> To carry out the movements of an often-practised drill
> Requiring speed and discipline, but not a lot of skill.
> They hoofed the ball, they packed the goal, their tactics were defined;
> And everybody wondered why attendances declined.

Money is, of course, the root of the evils which currently afflict soccer. Sadly, across the wide parameters of our beloved sport, we have allowed financial considerations and business acumen to dictate to the point where they are threatening the virtual extinction of the true spirit of the game.

As I see it football finds itself at a major crossroads. We either give the sport back to its most important participants—the players!—or, alternatively, stick doggedly to the present route which could lead to a possible soccer scenario where tiny radio receivers are stuck behind footballers' ears while the coach, from a seat in the directors' box, relays instructions to each member of his team in turn during the course of a game.

Sadly, this obsession with commercial gain, coupled with desperation to avoid the horrors which follow in the wake of a defeat, has transmitted itself to the players as well as to the men on the terracing. The fan violence which, particularly in England, has scarred the good name of the game in recent seasons, can be blamed on many things, but in part the wounds have been self-inflicted.

There is a lot wrong with football. But then, there is a lot wrong with society in general. Soccer will solve its own problems providing it changes course and sets off in a direction which will lead to a greater public awareness of what the game is really all about.

Having said that, I firmly believe that the basic skills are still around, albeit largely suppressed and lying latent below the surface. Given the chance and properly advised, the youngsters of today could disprove the old theory that they are nowhere near as talented as their counterparts of twenty, thirty or forty years ago. Football still manages to bring a warm glow to cold, icy winter afternoons and to produce stars of exceptional quality. Players like Davie Cooper, whose dazzling performances for Glasgow Rangers and Scotland in recent times have proved that all the coaching manuals in the world are no substitute for true skills. If there were a lot more Davie Coopers around, those menfolk who have deserted the terracings and now spend Saturday afternoons watching wrestling on the telly or shopping with the wife, would quickly give such mundane pastimes the elbow and return to the game in *really* significant numbers.

Although inclined to pour scorn on the efforts of club directors, I am well aware that a few of those high ranking individuals have contributed, and still contribute, a great deal to football in terms of financial support. Certainly many are much more interested in the status which comes with the job, revel in media exposure and have at least one eye on the effect which the position can have on their personal business interests. However, to take a swipe at directors in general is to serve a grave injustice upon the few who actually have

Davie Cooper . . . dazzling performances!

the welfare of their particular club at heart and whose actions as well as motives should be admired rather than condemned. Some have, admittedly, dug deeply into their pockets to plough much-needed capital into the game and, in doing so, have dragged more than one club back from the abyss of extinction. Such individuals are crucial to the future well-being of the sport. What a pity it is that such men of vision constitute the tiny minority of club directors!

Portraits of those footballers who have played fifty or more times for their country now hang in the offices of the Scottish Football Association in Glasgow and the sport's bosses in Scotland are to be applauded for this. But, unfortunately, the only people who will be able to cast their eyes on the paintings of such heroes as George Young and Willie Miller are the SFA staff, VIP guests and the office cleaner. In no way do I wish to seem churlish because I am genuinely delighted that these footballing greats are being honoured. It is undeniably a major step in the right direction. But is it not sad that so many great players are not represented? Players like Walter Arnott, Bob McPhail of Rangers, Celtic's Jimmy McGrory, George Cummings and many, many more. It wasn't their fault, after all, that such things as world wars and a dearth of international fixtures meant fewer caps in days when Scottish participation in tournaments such as the World Cup and European

Championships were beyond comprehension. Wouldn't it be wonderful if that much-mooted "Football Hall of Fame" could be built in Scotland? Somewhere of interest to take the kids on a wet Sunday afternoon instead of dragging them round some dingy old museum and art gallery, filled with stuffed animals and the works of little known artists. That tongue of mine is in the cheek again and I must remember that sarcasm is the lowest form of wit, mustn't I? But, in all seriousness, it would be marvellous if the money could be found to fund such an enterprise . . . wouldn't it?

Together, the Scottish Football Association, the Scottish League and the Scottish Professional Footballers' Association, in the shape of my big pal, Tony Higgins, could, with the backing of the local council, the business community and the football-loving public turn such a dream into reality! Many more people than visit those museums and art galleries would file through the doors and the token fee collected at the "gate" could be used to support and promote football at all levels, to ensure the welfare of past masters . . . to supply much-needed advice and financial assistance to any player forced to give up the game due to serious injury. Films, books, programmes, medals, photographs, caps and every type of football memorabilia which, otherwise, may be lost or melted down, could be saved! Even more cash would be generated through charging television and film companies for use of the premises for reference purposes or as a highly visual back-drop to some production. With a little imagination and a showbiz-type approach, rather than an austere, museum-like presentation, such a venture could generate enormous amounts of capital, thereby assuring the future well-being of the game. I am absolutely certain that, in soccer-mad Scotland, such a permanent exhibition would appeal to many more people than does the Burrell Collection, for instance. It would be an enormous attraction. Exiles and visitors from other countries would also flock to the place in their thousands, thereby supplying a very welcome boost to the Scottish tourist industry.

North of the border we never seem to tire of recalling that 5–1 "Wizards" victory in 1928. We are engulfed in a tide of emotion when remembering closely-fought Scottish victories in 1938, 1951, 1967 or 1977, for example. Yet we also would appear to be a nation of amnesiacs when anyone is unkind enough to bring up the subject of English victories at the same venue. We weren't really beaten 7–2 in 1955, were we? It is simply a figment of "Sassenach" imagination that the "Auld Enemy" annihilated our brave lads 9–3 in 1961. England won 5–1 in 1975? I can't remember that! Yes, disasters are too horrific to even contemplate and worthy only of being dispatched on the shortest possible route to the darkest recesses of any self-respecting Scotsman's mind.

But, hate the English? Not this fan. I adored Bobby Charlton almost as much as any footballer, despite the fact that I stood and watched this modern day "Hammer of the Scots" drill as many nails into the Scottish international football coffin as any other post-war player. Although they operated in the "enemy" camp, in retrospect I wouldn't have missed out on the privilege of witnessing the talents of white-shirted geniuses like Tom Finney, Johnny Haynes, Bobby Moore and Kevin Keegan for all the proverbial tea in China . . . even though those inconsiderate characters caused me considerable pain at the time!

For a man who absolutely hated to find himself on the losing side, Bill Shankly's attitude to the sport was the right one. "Shanks" knew better than anyone that it is the players and the fans who really matter. Renowned for his love of the game, sense of humour and admiration for that great Englishman, Tom Finney, Bill's very presence filled the air with an aura of his great love of football. Many tales have been told about the late, great Bill Shankly and his incomparable wit, but the one I like best is reputed to go something like this.

In the 1970s a talented young winger had broken into the England team and was the subject of rave notices in the sporting press. Eager to make his name, a hungry young reporter asked Shankly what he thought of the player, to which the great man replied: "The boy's an absolute genius, son . . . he's got everything . . . speed, ball control, bags of energy, goal-scoring flair and he knows how to head a ball." Praise indeed, and when the cub reporter remembered that Bill idolised Tom Finney, he asked "Shanks" how he felt the starlet's abilities stood in comparison with those of the ex-Preston and England star. "He's every bit as good as Finney, son," came the gruff and positive reply. Almost bursting with excitement and convinced he had obtained quotes which would make the following morning's sports' page headlines, the young journalist asked Shankly if he was actually saying that the player was as good as Finney. "Aye. A've told you, laddie . . . he's every bit as good," snorted the Liverpool manager, adding wryly as he turned away, "Mind you, son, I know it's hard to believe . . . but Tom's pushing sixty now." The reporter shuffled off somewhat deflated, realising that he had a lot to learn and that he had found himself on the receiving end of Shankly's tremendous wit.

Emotion . . . that's the key word when it comes to football! The joy which players experience in scoring a winning goal. The pain of defeat, which was never better illustrated than on the face of Scotland manager, Ally McLeod, in the wake of Scotland's failure to qualify for the latter stages of the 1978 World Cup in Argentina. Emotions on the terracings, in the stands and on the field of play, as hopes are dashed and then renewed in a whirlpool of tension, joy, despair, laughter and tears. Tempers become frayed and reach breaking point. Hearts are shattered in defeat and the pleasure of victory brings with it a sense of well-being which is beyond description. Love it or hate it, football simply cannot be ignored. Its kingdom stretches across the

Before and after Scotland's 1978 World Cup trip to Argentina, as mirrored on the face of manager, Ally McLeod. Thankfully he always bounces back . . . guys like Ally have a tremendous amount to contribute to the game.

broad spectrum of society—rich and poor, young and old, politicians and preachers—and the only losers are those who have never fallen under its magical and hypnotic spell!

One man who was captivated by the sport at an early age is Dr Runcie, Archbishop of Canterbury and head of the Church of England. I am very grateful to the Archbishop for taking the time to reply to my letter and for contributing the ensuing recollections of the part which soccer played in his childhood:

"What's the joke . . . don't you know football's a serious business these days?" Neil Kinnock, leader of the Labour Party, is in stitches at this Hearts match but Wallace Mercer (left) and Sandy Jardine (right) don't seem to have anything to laugh about.

Dr Runcie, Archbishop of Canterbury.

I was mad about football and liked nothing better than going with my father to watch the local team play. It was a great thrill to be taken to see my side, Liverpool, and, occasionally, I would also watch Everton who had a marvellous centre-forward called "Dixie" Dean. My father, however, was a Scot from Kilmarnock. Our family were really living in exile on Merseyside and he was always talking about Scottish football. Most of my aunts and uncles were scattered around Scotland. My father still supported Kilmarnock and promised me that, one day, he would take me to see some *real* football. He kept that promise and, while on a visit to Scotland, I remember going with him to Rugby Park some time in the early 1930s. Kilmarnock were playing Rangers and won! This was largely thanks to a superb centre-forward called Buddie Maxwell. I can still recall that he was a great favourite with the crowd . . . "Shove it doon the gulley, Buddie," they cried.

That soccer-mad youngster could never have envisaged the role he was to fulfil later in life!

Football has certainly been the axle around which much of my life has pivoted. It's not far short of forty years since a little brat of a laddie still to master the art of joined-up writing first sampled the unique taste and smell of the terracings! The days when I wiped my nose on a sleeve, collected beer bottles and dreamed of being a great player are gone forever and, somehow, that little "ugly duckling" of the school playground never turned into a beautiful swan . . . just an "attic fanatic" who has an abiding obsession with an unbeatable ball game!

I would love to be afforded the opportunity of stepping back in time to watch the dashing wing play of Johnny Ferguson, the defensive qualities of those "giants", Walter Arnott and George Cummings, as well as the guile and sheer brilliance of classical inside-forwards such as Scotland's Alex James, Ireland's Peter Doherty and the golden-haired Wilf Mannion of Middlesbrough and England fame. Unfortunately, the only fellow I've heard of who owns a time machine is Dr Who and, knowing that I would have endless football worlds to explore, it is inconceivable that he would be over-eager to lend it to the likes of me. I can only dream of the exploits of those great players born too early to enable me to see them play and be eternally grateful for the contribution which they made to the greatest of games.

The souvenirs lovingly crammed between the rafters in that loft of mine represent a lifetime of collecting soccer memorabilia. It's a haven where countless memories come flooding back. The many thousands of programmes, photographs, books, badges and miles of film footage, rescued from an incinerator, will still be around when this lad is long gone. My greatest wish is that those treasured mementoes will play their part in keeping the names of past masters alive.

Perhaps, as many never cease to point out, I am too wrapped up in a love affair with the game. Maybe I am inclined to get carried away and allow enthusiasm to cloud my sense of judgment. But I need apologise to no one because, throughout the years, I have met a wide range of folk from all walks of life and, much more often than not, it is the true enthusiasts who are the most interesting characters, whatever their particular hobby or passion may be! It should be remembered that many people who have contributed something of lasting value have, in their day, been regarded as eccentrics.

The frequent use of adjectives such as great, glorious and wonderful throughout the pages of this book is, quite simply, indicative of a great love of football and the players who made it. And what on earth can be wrong with that? Perhaps, to coin a well known phrase, I am, in conventional terms, "not in possession of the full shilling" when it comes to my approach to football. However, on looking around and seeing some of those who readily conform to mediocrity, outwardly appear rich and successful, but have stabbed others in the back to achieve their miserable ambitions . . . all I can say is "Thank God I'm a failure and a nonconformist!"

One way or another football has always evoked a highly emotional response. From the very dawn of time when our ape-like ancestors first kicked a stone . . . on through those difficult days of repression in the Middle Ages . . . and on again to that occasion in 1815 when the game was just beginning to become accepted and Sir Walter Scott, along with 2,000 others, was witness to a match played between over one hundred men from Selkirk and a similar number from Yarrow. The players were almost indistinguishable from the crowd in a "sport" where kicking, handling and almost any means of achieving victory was permissible . . . onwards, ever onwards, into the Victorian age and the beginnings of football as we know it today . . . then into that golden era of the gigantic crowds in the 1930s . . . and so to our own time when man first walked on the moon, television satellites high up among the heavens beam football into homes in all corners of the globe and footballers can cost millions of pounds. This is one helluva ball game!

I have a dream that, one fine day, football will free itself of the "winner takes all" attitude as well as the greed and hypocrisy which are so harmful to the sport . . . I have a dream that in footballing days to come there will be a far greater awareness and appreciation of the contribution made by those giants of yesteryear . . . I have a dream that the fans of Glasgow Rangers and Glasgow Celtic, for example, will bury those idiotic hatchets of religious bigotry and mingle together in harmony, appreciating and applauding the skills of any player, whatever his denomination or the colour of the jersey he is wearing . . . I have a dream that, at least once in a soccer-crazed existence, my lovely old Hibernian will win the Scottish Cup . . . I have a dream that, wherever it is played, football will always prosper and flourish. A vision which will become an everlasting reality if everyone who cares about this magnificent obsession of ours remembers those splendid words which Johnny McDowall, Secretary of the Scottish Football Association, penned shortly before his death in 1928:

> When the last great scorer
> Comes to write against his name
> He'll write, not that he won or lost
> But how he played the game.

Yes, it's always nice to win. But how much more rewarding and meaningful when victory is achieved with style and sportsmanship. That's the very stuff that dreams are made of!

The author (centre) and that highly esteemed writer/broadcaster, Bob Crampsey, (back row on right) put on a very happy face when photographed with some stars of yesteryear. The players (back row left to right): Willie Toner, Kilmarnock and Scotland, John McPhail, Celtic and Scotland, Jimmy Davidson, Partick Thistle and Scotland and Jimmy Mitchell, Aberdeen and the Scottish League. (Front row left to right): Willie Redpath, Motherwell and Scotland, Bobby Flavell, Airdrie and Scotland, Bobby Shearer, Rangers and Scotland and Tommy Ring, Clyde and Scotland.